THE NEW BIG BOOK OF
AMERICA

By Todd Davis and Marc Frey

COURAGE
BOOKS

AN IMPRINT OF RUNNING PRESS
PHILADELPHIA • LONDON

© 2002 by Running Press
All rights reserved under the Pan-American and International Copyright Conventions

Printed in China

9 8 7 6 5

Digit on the right indicates the number of this printing

Library of Congress Cataloging-in-Publication Number is 2001094087
ISBN 0-7624-1263-1

Cover designed by Bill Jones
Interior designed by Frank Punzo
Edited by Greg Jones
Photo research by Susan Oyama

This book may be ordered from the publisher.
But try your bookstore first!

Published by Courage Books, an imprint of
Running Press Book Publishers
125 South Twenty-Second Street
Philadelphia, Pennsylvania 19103–4399

Visit us on the web!
www.runningpress.com

Table of Contents

INTRODUCTION

Diverse Peoples, Common Values

America has always been a compelling but complex idea, an inviting yet challenging landscape. The earliest Europeans to settle along the Atlantic Coast came with hopes of economic success and spiritual salvation. Some people realized their dreams; others faced ongoing struggles. While plantation owners and enterprising merchants became rich and powerful, colonists of more modest means suffered many deprivations—famine and disease among them. American Indians and African slaves faced even harsher circumstances. Native Americans lost treasured lands to the settlers and died in large numbers from imported European diseases. Slaves worked long hours in poor conditions without basic rights and freedoms. The Declaration of Independence and the United States Constitution changed the American experience, creating a society based on important concepts like freedom, equality, and responsibility. Although these ideas meant different things to different people, they comprised a common and flexible framework that provided for both fervent debate and domestic stability.

Until the mid-nineteenth century, familiar tensions and conflicts continued to shape American life. Determined settlers moved westward across North America, and an expanding industrial economy generated great wealth for enterprising businessmen. But many people did not share in this prosperity. The majority of European immigrants—whose work in factories and rail yards fueled America's growth—often faced dire circumstances. Native Americans lost increasing amounts of land, and African-American slaves continued to live without freedom. Indeed, passionate debates about slavery divided the North and the South during this era.

The Civil War, however, fundamentally changed national life—in many ways it represented a second American Revolution. Although the war did not resolve all of America's problems, the Union victory caused people to accept broader definitions of freedom, equality, and responsibility. This change enabled African Americans, women, immigrants, and other disadvantaged groups to experience the fruits of American prosperity and freedom. As time passed, more people lived fuller lives.

As the twentieth century progressed, Americans continued to refine the principles upon which the country was established. The suffering associated with the Great Depression of the 1930s exposed flaws in the American way of life, demonstrating that all citizens could plummet into hardship and suggesting that the government should do more to help the American people. As the Depression waned, the United States fought World War II in defense of freedom and equality. The war effort convinced many citizens that more people should benefit from these concepts. From the late 1950s to the early 1970s, many Americans—including African Americans, women, Native Americans, and immigrants—participated in a variety of social-protest movements

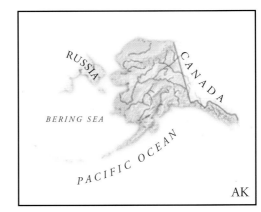

AK

that deeply affected national life. Although Americans continue to argue about how the government should protect and preserve national values, most agree that all citizens deserve equality of opportunity and freedom of expression.

Sectional Conflicts and National Unity

After the Civil War unified the North and the South, other regional conflicts came to the forefront. Throughout the nineteenth century, for example, the West and the East battled over how to divide the fruits of America's economy. Many western workers and farmers wanted a more humane economy, but eastern financial elites sought to maximize profits in the name of national progress. Reformers from both regions eventually helped construct a national economy that protected the interests of westerners and easterners alike. Their efforts further solidified the bonds that bind Americans together.

During the twentieth century, the Great Depression, World War II, and the Cold War further demonstrated the need for an enduring national unity. These events helped forge an American identity that overwhelmed regional loyalties, joining all Americans in common cause. Technological developments like radio, television, and film were especially instrumental in fostering a national culture. And at the beginning of the twenty-first century, advancements such as e-mail and the Internet continue to bring people closer together. As the world becomes a smaller and more interdependent place, Americans' understanding of freedom, equality, and responsibility make residents of each state part of an important national community. American citizens share memories of a common past and dreams of a brighter future.

ALABAMA

Nickname: Heart of Dixie | **Capital:** Montgomery | **Statehood:** December 14, 1819 (22nd)
Population: 4,369,862 (23rd) | **Area:** 52,423 sq. mi. (30th) | **Highest point:** 2,405 ft. (Mt. Cheaha)

Alabama's topography is notably diverse. The plateaus of the Appalachian Highlands in the northeast gradually slope southward to the rich land of the Black Belt. Named for its fertile dark soil, this gently rolling lowland sustained the cotton-producing economy and culture that was vital to the state's development. Near the Gulf of Mexico, the swampy delta of the Mobile River contains a variety of lush flora, including blossoming azaleas and moss-draped oaks.

Originally explored by the Spanish in the early sixteenth century and colonized by French traders in 1702, Alabama was controlled by several Indian tribes until the early nineteenth century. In the decades preceding the Civil War, nearly half of Alabama's population consisted of slaves who worked the state's vast cotton plantations. Following the South's defeat in the Civil War, Alabama refused to grant freed slaves citizenship rights and, along with nine other states, was placed under military rule until 1868. For the next century, African-Americans struggled economically as sharecroppers and tenant farmers, and did not have any political power.

In the post-World War II period, Alabama became the center of the emerging civil rights movement. In 1955 Rosa Parks—a black member of the NAACP (National Association for the Advancement of Colored People)—challenged the state's segregation policy by refusing to give up her seat on a Montgomery bus. Following her arrest, Martin Luther King Jr. led a successful yearlong boycott of the buses. In 1961 "freedom riders"—groups of black and white people who protested segregation by riding buses together—were met by violent mobs in Birmingham and Montgomery. Two years later, Birmingham police commissioner Eugene "Bull" Connor turned fire hoses and police dogs on black protesters; Governor George C. Wallace attempted to stop the integration of the University of Alabama; and Ku Klux Klan members dynamited an African-American Birmingham church, killing four young girls. The violent white response to black direct-action increased public support for civil rights and forced the federal government to confront the issues of injustice and racism in the South. In 1965 King led a march from Selma to Montgomery to protest restrictions on black voters. Montgomery is now home to the Civil Rights Memorial, which honors those who gave their lives in support of the movement.

Helen Keller (1880–1968)

When she was less than two years old, Helen Keller contracted an illness that left her blind and deaf. Because she could not hear, she found it very difficult to speak. Just before Keller's seventh birthday, Anne Sullivan—who also was blind—arrived at her Alabama home to tutor her. With Sullivan's patient assistance, Keller learned to speak, read in Braille, and write on a specially constructed typewriter. After

graduating from college with honors and publishing *The Story of My Life*, Keller traveled and lectured throughout the world. A passionate advocate for other people with disabilities, she also campaigned on behalf of civil rights, women's suffrage, and world peace. Because she overcame such considerable odds, Keller remains an inspiration for all Americans.

Jesse Owens (1913–1980)

One of the greatest athletes of all time, Alabama native James Cleveland Owens proved to the world that African Americans could excel among white athletes. While in high school and college, Owens broke several track-and-field world records. A member of the U.S. track team at the 1936 Olympics, held in Berlin, Owens won four gold medals and set three Olympic records. His brilliant performances contradicted German leader Adolph Hitler's false claims about the superiority of the Aryan (white) race. After retiring from competition, Owens played an active role in developing youth athletic programs. In 1976 President Gerald R. Ford awarded him the Medal of Freedom in recognition of his contributions to American life.

ALASKA

Nickname: Last Frontier | **Capital:** Juneau | **Statehood:** January 3, 1959 (49th)
Population: 619,500 (48th) | **Area:** 656,424 sq. mi. (1st) | **Highest point:** 20,320 ft. (Mount McKinley)

A massive state bordering the Pacific Ocean, the Bering Sea, the Arctic Ocean, and Canada, Alaska has both polar and temperate regions. Most of its residents live near the cities of Anchorage and Fairbanks, although small villages thrive throughout the state. Fishing and mining dominate Alaska's economy. Fishermen catch mostly salmon along with a variety of crabs. Miners dig gold, silver, and coal from the earth. And drillers extract huge quantities of oil and natural gas, shipping it to the lower forty-eight states. Tourists also flock to Alaska to enjoy its tall mountains, vast wilderness, clear waters, and abundant wildlife.

A number of native peoples still populate Alaska, including the Tlingit, Tinneh, Aleuts, and Eskimos. Europeans arrived during the eighteenth century, sparking a fervent battle over land rights with the native population that continues today. Russians also came to Alaska during the eighteenth century, crossing over the Bering Strait and declaring ownership of the land. They developed a fur trade that linked Alaska to Asia, Europe, and North America's Pacific Coast. The United States purchased Alaska from Russia in 1867 for $7.2 million, although many Americans thought of Alaska as a great wasteland.

When pioneers discovered gold in Alaska in the late nineteenth century, prospectors rushed to the area with hopes of making their fortunes in the last American frontier. In order to speed travel within the region, workers built the Alaska Railroad and the Alaska Highway. When petroleum companies discovered large oil deposits in the early twentieth century, they began to drill in a number of locations, eventually focusing their projects in Prudhoe Bay and building a 789-mile pipeline that transports oil to Valdez Harbor. From there, companies ship Alaskan oil to the rest of the United States, making the state a prime source of American energy. But such heavy energy development has damaged Alaska's pristine environment and wildlife. In 1989 the oil tanker Exxon Valdez ran aground, causing an environmental disaster by spilling 11 million gallons of crude oil near Prince William Sound. People and politicians continue to battle over the development of Alaska and its effect on the environment. Although Americans feared they had purchased a useless tract of land in 1867, the state and its peoples have enriched the American way of life.

Environmentalism

A political philosophy based on the belief that people need to conserve the earth's natural resources, environmentalism has become a strong force in contemporary American—and especially Alaskan—life. Although conservationists like John Wesley Powell and Theodore Roosevelt had encouraged people to value the land and create nature preserves during the late 1800s and early 1900s, environmentalism gained momentum after 1962. That year, biologist Rachel Carson published the best-selling book, *Silent Spring*, which warned Americans that pollution stemming from population growth and agricultural practices threatened to poison the earth's land, oceans, and air. Although Carson died before her ideas gained widespread attention, her work is still influential. Those who currently oppose oil drilling in Alaska's Arctic National Wildlife Refuge draw on her philosophies.

Rachel Carson

Seward's Folly

In 1867 Secretary of State William Seward arranged for the United States to purchase Alaska from Russia. Many Americans thought Seward was crazy to pay more than $7 million for the huge and unexplored territory, and the deal was referred to as "Seward's Folly." But the purchase has since paid for itself many times over.

When the rich fisheries off Alaska's coast and the oil reserves under Alaska's soil proved extremely lucrative many years later, Seward looked like a genius in retrospect. Like the Louisiana Purchase more than sixty years earlier, the purchase of Alaska helped pave the way for American power and prosperity.

William H. Seward

ARIZONA

Nickname: Grand Canyon State | **Capital:** Phoenix | **Statehood:** February 14, 1912 (48th)
Population: 4,778,332 (20th) | **Area:** 114,006 sq. mi. (6th) | **Highest Point:** 12,633 ft. (Humphreys Peak)

The name "Arizona" comes from an Indian word meaning "place of the young spring." Although the state is known for its cactus deserts, northern Arizona is cool and blanketed with pine trees. Farming, ranching, mining, and lumbering dominated Arizona's economy before World War II, but industries like electronics, communications, and aeronautics soon grew strong. Indeed, Arizonans have helped to spark America's economic transformation during the information age.

Spaniards explored the region during the sixteenth century, and the area became part of Mexico after 1821. Following the Mexican-American War in 1848, the United States claimed Arizona and made it part of the New Mexico Territory. White settlers soon came into conflict with the Apache Indians, who had inhabited the area for centuries. The Chiricahua—the most nomadic and aggressive Apache group—reached an accord with the U.S. Government in 1858, but war broke out three years later. Led by Chief Cochise, Chiricahua bands bedeviled the scattered American troops and took control of Arizona in 1862 while most

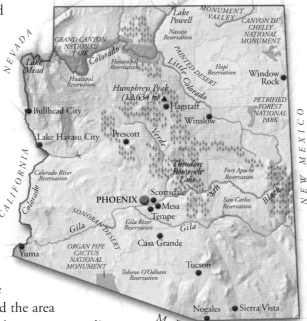

U.S. soldiers were engaged in the Civil War. After the Union victory in 1865, the Apache War resumed. Cochise held out until 1871 by leading raids from his stronghold in the Dragoon Mountains. When Cochise surrendered, another Chiricahua warrior, Geronimo, continued resistance until he finally surrendered in 1886.

One of the fastest growing states in the nation, Arizona absorbs immigrants from across the United States and Mexico. Drawn by the state's warm weather, large numbers of senior citizens move to Arizona to reside in settlements like Sun City and Green Valley.

Arizonans have supported a conservative brand of politics for years, backing Republican stars like Barry Goldwater and John McCain. Robust and handsome, Goldwater and McCain symbolize the rugged individualism and pioneer values that define the West's mythic reputation.

Arizona is also a popular tourist destination, with more than 5 million people visiting the Grand Canyon each year. Located in the northwest corner of the state, the Grand Canyon is 217 miles long, one mile deep, and up to eighteen miles wide. Its spectacular vistas, along with the challenging outdoor activities associated with it, have awed tourists for generations. It contributes to Arizona's unique appeal.

Western Conservatism

In response to the Great Depression, American politicians came to accept an expanded definition of federal power that allowed the U.S. government to regulate industry and supervise programs designed to enhance the "general welfare." During the 1960s, however, a conservative brand of politics flourished in the American West. Arizona Senator Barry Goldwater based his 1964 presidential campaign on policies designed to shrink the central government, preserve traditional morality, and oppose the spread of communism. Goldwater lost but, in 1966, Ronald Reagan became governor of California by championing similar ideas. When Reagan won two presidential elections in 1980 and 1984, conservative politics were ascendant.

Barry Goldwater (left)

Geronimo (1829–1909)

A Chiricahua Apache war leader, Geronimo's real name was Goyathlay, which means "one who yawns." He became a renowned warrior after Mexican soldiers killed his mother, wife, and children in 1858. He led many raids into Mexico and, after the Civil War, fought scores of battles with the U.S. Army. In what was then called the "Department of Arizona," Geronimo fought settlers who moved into Apache territory and soldiers who wanted to place his people on a reservation. He briefly agreed to live on a reservation in 1884, but—along with several followers—fled the area a year later. Geronimo finally surrendered in 1886, and the Army deported him to Oklahoma. He never saw Arizona again.

ARKANSAS

Nickname: Land of Opportunity | **Capital:** Little Rock | June 15th, 1836 (25th)
Population: 2,551,373 (33rd) | **Area:** 53,182 sq. mi. (29th) | **Highest point:** 2,753 ft. (Magazine Mt.)

The high Ozark and Ouachita Mountains—made of ancient sandstone and limestone—dominate Arkansas's northwest landscape. Several rivers slice through its rich agricultural valleys and flow into the Mississippi River. Among the nation's leading producers of cotton, rice, and poultry, Arkansas also yields large quantities of oil, natural gas, and bromine. Little Rock, the capital, is the commercial center of the state. Its cosmopolitan character is symbolic of Arkansas's growing urbanization.

The first permanent European settlement in Arkansas served as a fur-trading center and a way station for travelers between the Gulf of Mexico and the Great Lakes. However, conflict between whites and Native Americans hindered widespread settlement—at the time of the Louisiana Purchase, Arkansas had only a few hundred white residents. But by 1820 Arkansas had drawn enough people to become a territory; its northern boundary marked the line of the Missouri Compromise (1820) that separated the slave and free states.

In the years leading up to the Civil War, Arkansas's population boomed and slavery spread as plantation owners developed the rich cotton lands of the southern and eastern sections of the state. Although strong Unionist feeling in the mountainous northwest (where there were few slaves) postponed secession, Arkansas ultimately joined the Confederacy. For the next century, Arkansas experienced slow economic development and remained predominantly rural.

In 1957 the city of Little Rock drew worldwide attention when nine black students attempted to enroll in Central High School. Until that time only white students had attended the school, despite a 1954 Supreme Court decision that outlawed segregation. White resistance to integration, led by Governor Orval E. Faubus, forced President Dwight Eisenhower to send in the National Guard. Under the Guard's protection, the "Little Rock Nine" completed the school year. In the 1960s Arkansas gradually achieved integration. In recent years, the state has enjoyed considerable growth and economic renewal. The economy of the Ozark region especially has been transformed by the proliferation of Arkansas-native Sam Walton's Wal-Mart discount chain stores.

J. William Fulbright (1905–1995)

A graduate of the University of Arkansas, J. William Fulbright returned there in 1939 to become its president. Elected to the Senate from Arkansas in 1944, he sponsored legislation that provided funds for the exchange of students between the United States and other countries. His fifteen-year tenure as the influential chairman of the Senate Foreign Relations Committee was marked by notable cases of dissent. In 1961 he objected to the Bay of Pigs invasion. By 1966, Fulbright had emerged as a powerful critic of the Vietnam War. That year, he began investigations into American actions in Southeast Asia. Denouncing the "arrogance of power" that increasingly had come to characterize American foreign policy, Fulbright sharply questioned President Lyndon Johnson's advisors about the war. These televised hearings helped crystallize American antiwar sentiment.

Hillary Rodham Clinton (b. 1947)

Born in Chicago, Hillary Rodham graduated from Wellesley College before enrolling at Yale Law School. There she met Bill Clinton, a fellow law student. They married and moved to Arkansas, where Hillary became a high-powered Little Rock lawyer and an advocate for children's welfare. Following Bill Clinton's victory in the 1992 presidential election, Hillary made clear that she would be more than a ceremonial First Lady. In 1993, for example, she headed a task force on national health-care reform. Although her policy work drew criticism, Hillary was a powerful symbol of the changing role and status of women in American society. In 2000, she captured one of New York's U.S. Senate seats, making her the first First Lady to be elected to office in her own right.

CALIFORNIA

Nickname: Golden State | **Capital:** Sacramento | **Statehood:** September 9, 1850 (31st)
Population: 33,145,121 (1st) | **Area:** 163,707 sq. mi. (3rd) | **Highest point:** 14,494 ft. (Mount Whitney)

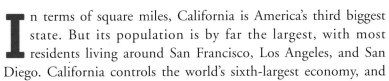

In terms of square miles, California is America's third biggest state. But its population is by far the largest, with most residents living around San Francisco, Los Angeles, and San Diego. California controls the world's sixth-largest economy, and agricultural enterprises yield much of its wealth. The state's unrivalled entertainment industry captures the public's imagination both in America and abroad. Disneyland draws millions of tourists each year, and Hollywood generates much of the world's feature films and television programs.

Spaniards first explored the California coast in the sixteenth century and, during the next hundred years, established religious missions across the territory. Priests converted thousands of Indians to Christianity while becoming economic moguls, controlling massive herds of cattle, horses, and sheep. But the Indians did not fare as well; colonists carried diseases that killed three-quarters of the region's Native Americans.

Descendants of the original Spanish colonists (called californios) controlled California during the early nineteenth century and, when the Mexican-American War exploded in 1846, they fought against U.S. troops. However, American settlers sparked a rebellion of their own and declared an independent California republic. All of the state's residents ultimately accepted U.S. authority when Mexico ceded the area to America in 1848.

When prospectors discovered gold that same year, Americans rushed into the area in amazing numbers to seek their fortunes. Even after the gold rush peaked in 1852, Americans continued to flock to the Golden State. As time passed, California became an agricultural marvel. Farm workers and landowners, however, had fitful relations. Chinese and Japanese laborers worked the land dutifully with little economic reward. In fact, laws were enacted to restrict Chinese immigration (1882) and prevent Japanese land ownership (1913). Agricultural unrest peaked during the 1960s when Cesar Chavez organized the United Farmworkers of America in order to improve working conditions and boost workers' wages.

Filled with Asian Americans, African Americans, Mexican Americans, Native Americans, Whites, and other peoples, California is a microcosm of America's diverse population. Its teeming cities highlight the nation's ability to accommodate immigrants, and its sunny beaches evoke images of prosperity and pleasure.

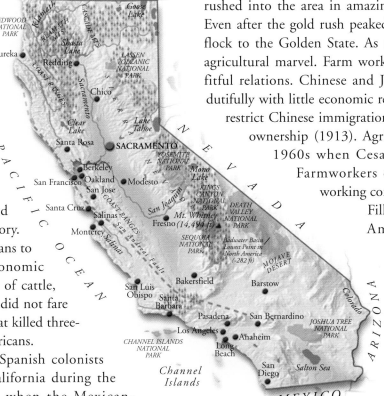

The San Francisco Earthquake of 1906

On April 18, 1906, a massive earthquake struck San Francisco and destroyed much of the city. The initial quake lasted for nearly one minute and was felt across California and in nearby states like Oregon and Nevada. A fire quickly engulfed the city's many wooden buildings, and more than 2,000 people died as a result. Scientists of this era did not understand why the earthquake occurred, but the earthquake created a scientific advance by drawing attention to "plate tectonics." In the wake of the San Francisco Earthquake, people came to understand that when the massive plates on which the world's continents rest move together, they create stresses that generate earthquakes.

Hollywood

A municipal district located northwest of Los Angeles, Hollywood became the center of America's motion picture industry during the early twentieth century. After 1915, movie executives like Cecil B. DeMille, Jesse Lansky, and Samuel Goldwyn opened studios in the area and generated a wave of films that helped define the culture of the United States. As people across the nation watched these movies, their common cultural reference points increased. During the 1960s, television became especially powerful, and Hollywood became home to much of this new industry. Hollywood Boulevard continues to attract tourists interested in catching a glimpse of America's entertainment elite. And Hollywood still represents the grandeur of American power and wealth.

Actor Tom Cruise

COLORADO

Nickname: Centennial State | **Capital:** Denver | **Statehood:** August 1, 1876 (38th)
Population: 4,056,133 (24th) | **Area:** 104,100 sq. mi. (8th) | **Highest point:** 14,433 ft. (Mount Elbert)

Decorated with the majestic Rocky Mountains, Colorado contains a stunning variety of natural resources, animal life, and vegetation. Farms and ranches produce grains, pork, and beef. The people of Denver, Fort Collins, and Colorado Springs work in industries like publishing, food processing, paper production, and munitions development. But the state's principal contribution to the American economy involves energy production. Colorado's rivers and dams generate needed hydroelectric power, and Denver marks the center of the interior West's coal and shale oil industries.

Indian tribes—including the Arapaho, Cheyenne, and Utes—populated Colorado before European explorers arrived. During the nineteenth century, Spaniards came to the area from Mexico because they believed Colorado contained a magical city of gold and silver (often called El Dorado). Americans also explored Colorado at this time. Indians helped legendary figures like Zebulon Pike, Kit Carson, and Jim Bridger traverse the region. These helpful Native Americans, however, fell victim to their own generosity when

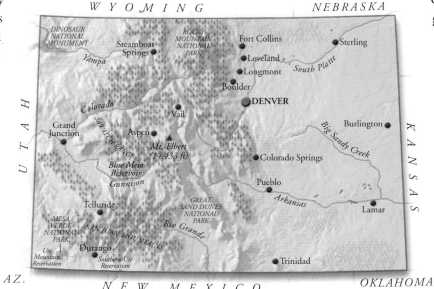

White settlers—who possessed no legal land claims—began to displace them. In 1859 prospectors discovered gold in Colorado and settlers started building boomtowns across the state. Most of these towns disappeared after the gold rush collapsed in the 1890s, but cattle ranchers, mining companies, and land speculators replenished the area's non-native population.

As settlers poured into Colorado, the American government sent surveyors into the area to plan the development of the West. Politicians hoped to devise a land-distribution system that drained population westward, placing poor people from the East on western lands. This plan failed miserably. Nevertheless, later planners based the complicated land laws that still shape western life on what surveyors tried to do in Colorado.

Ski resorts like Aspen and Vail receive thousands of visitors each winter, while summertime adventure seekers go white-water rafting on the state's rivers. Scenic and accessible, Colorado attracts great numbers of tourists throughout all four seasons.

John Wesley Powell (1834–1902)

A famed geologist, ethnologist, and anthropologist, John Wesley Powell helped Americans understand western lands and the people who populated them. After fighting in the Union Army during the Civil War, Powell directed a federal geological survey in Colorado and other western territories

that encouraged the government to develop the region with an eye toward conservation. His conservationist ideas set him apart from his peers, many of whom believed that the West should become a playground for profit-minded businessmen. Powell also developed an appreciation of Indian cultures and wrote a catalog of Indian languages that remains useful to this day.

The Gold Rush

In January 1848 a New Jersey mechanic named John Marshal discovered gold while building a sawmill for John Sutter near what is now Sacramento, California. Word of his discovery quickly spread across the United States, and thousands of Americans risked their lives to cross the continent and win their fortunes. Although many fortune-seekers died along the way, their deaths did not deter a later group of prospectors who, in 1859, traveled to Colorado after local miners discovered rich gold deposits. Farmers, ranchers, and businessmen soon followed prospectors into Colorado, populating the area for the first time and linking it to the national economy.

CONNECTICUT

Nickname: Constitution State | **Capital:** Hartford | **Statehood:** January 9, 1788 (5th)
Population: 3,282,031 (29th) | **Area:** 5,544 sq. mi. (48th) | **Highest Point:** 2,380 ft. (Mount Frissell)

Roughly rectangular in shape, Connecticut takes its name from an Algonquin Indian word meaning, "land on the long tidal river." A blend of modern urban (and suburban) development and rustic landscapes that maintains the charm of colonial New England, Connecticut displays sharp contrasts between areas of great wealth and deep poverty.

Throughout the colonial period, Connecticut remained an agricultural region with a few small towns such as Hartford and New Haven. Because its fast-flowing streams and waterfalls could be easily harnessed for power, Connecticut led the nation into the industrial revolution. Cities and towns in the state were famous for the goods they produced. Many industrial advances were made possible in part by the ingenuity of some important Connecticut residents. In the 1790s Eli Terry began producing machine-made clocks. Eli Whitney, famous for his invention of the cotton gin in 1794, helped develop the modern system of mass production, using interchangeable parts to manufacture guns. Weapons produced in Connecticut—

such as Colt and Winchester firearms—were used to fight the nation's wars throughout the nineteenth and twentieth centuries. Following World War II, new military products were developed in Connecticut; a Groton shipyard launched the world's first nuclear-powered submarine in 1954. In addition to munitions, Connecticut is home to America's insurance industry. Dating from the eighteenth century when marine insurance was underwritten to cover the hazards of shipping, Connecticut insurance companies now issue a variety of policies for millions of Americans.

For the past several decades, Connecticut has been one of the nation's richest states. Many major corporations, especially in the defense and financial-services industries, moved their headquarters to the state's southwest corner, near New York City. However, Connecticut's three largest cities—Bridgeport, Hartford, and New Haven—remained among America's poorest. In recent years, the state has made efforts to rebuild urban neighborhoods and better enable all residents to share in its prosperity.

The Hartford Convention

On December 14, 1814, members of the Federalist Party from the six New England states attended a convention in Hartford, Connecticut to protest the War of 1812 between the United States and Great Britain. The New England Federalists opposed the war because it hurt the fishing industry and overseas commerce. A rumor soon spread that the delegates were contemplating secession from the Union. Although untrue, the rumor irreparably damaged the reputation of the party, which was already unpopular with the majority of American citizens. As a result, the party of Alexander Hamilton and John Adams did not survive the presidential election of 1816.

Harriet Beecher Stowe (1811–1896)

Born into a prominent Connecticut family, Harriet Beecher grew up as a minister's daughter and developed strong religious beliefs. When her family moved to Cincinnati, Ohio in 1832, Harriet visited Kentucky plantations and became a strong opponent of slavery as a result. After marrying Calvin Stowe and raising six children, she wrote *Uncle Tom's Cabin* in 1852. Dramatizing the evils of slavery and depicting blacks as heroic figures, this novel sold more than one million copies and strengthened the abolitionist movement in the United States. In 1856 Stowe wrote a second antislavery novel, *Dred, A Tale of the Great Dismal Swamp*, and became an American celebrity.

DELAWARE

Nickname: First State | **Capital:** Dover | **Statehood:** December 7, 1787 (1st)
Population: 753,538 (45th) | **Area:** 2,489 sq. mi. (49th) | **Highest point:** 448 ft. (Ebright Road)

Delaware occupies a small niche in America's northeastern urban corridor. Extensive saltwater marshes fringe the shores of the Delaware River and Delaware Bay. Further south, the coast is characterized by dunes and long sandy beaches. More than two-thirds of the population lives in and around Wilmington, its largest city. The northern part of the state supports an enormous chemical industry and provides a home to hundreds of corporations and banks. Southern Delaware remains largely rural and lightly settled. Its farmers raise chickens, along with a wide range of agricultural products, for markets throughout the Northeast.

Delaware takes its name from Thomas West, Third Baron De La Warr, Virginia's first colonial governor. Like other Middle-Atlantic states, the colonial population of Delaware was varied; it included Swedes, Finns, Dutch, English, and French settlers. Following the American Revolution, Delaware's residents actively supported the movement for a strong national government. Quickly calling a state convention at Dover in December 1787, Delaware became the first state to ratify the Constitution.

As national political parties arose, Delaware supported the Federalists, adhering to the party of Alexander Hamilton and John Adams well into the 1820s. A slaveholding border state, it later supported the Democratic Party; antislavery Republican candidate Abraham Lincoln did not carry Delaware in 1860 or 1864. Because of its extensive economic ties to the North, however, Delaware remained loyal to the Union during the Civil War. Fort Delaware, on Pea Patch Island in the Delaware River, served as a prison for captured Confederate soldiers.

In the second half of the nineteenth century, industry expanded rapidly in the northern part of the state. The Wilmington area attracted immigrants from Ireland, Germany, Italy, Poland, and Russia. Most of these immigrants went to work manufacturing chemicals. In 1802 Eleuthère Irénée du Pont de Nemours, a French immigrant, had established a gunpowder mill on Brandywine Creek near Wilmington. His firm supplied nearly all the military explosives used by the United States in its wars. Now known simply as "Du Pont," it has evolved into one of the largest chemical companies in the world. The company's profits have funded many charitable works.

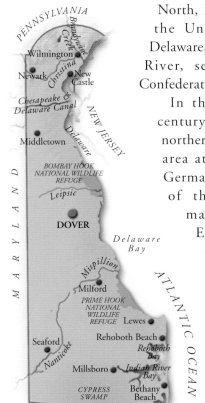

Non-English Exploration of North America

Between 1614 and 1620, several Dutch ships explored the Delaware River looking for the fabled Northwest Passage through North America to the Pacific Ocean. Initially, the Dutch were more interested in trade than colonization. In 1638 a Swedish expedition set up the first permanent settlement in the state—called "New Sweden"—on the site of present-day Wilmington. Over the next two decades, the Dutch and the Swedes fought for control of the area. Under the leadership of Peter Stuyvesant, governor of New Netherland, the Dutch ended Swedish rule in North America in 1655. Less than twenty years later, the English permanently displaced the Dutch in Delaware and throughout the mid-Atlantic region.

Caesar Rodney (1728–1784)

In 1774 and 1775 Delaware sent three of its most prominent citizens—Caesar Rodney, George Read, and Thomas McKean—to the First and Second Continental Congresses in Philadelphia. In July 1776 Delaware's delegation was divided over whether to support the Declaration of Independence. Read opposed a declaration, believing it to be too drastic a step; McKean and Rodney supported it, but Rodney was home in Delaware at the time. Summoned by McKean via a messenger, Rodney rode all night on horseback—through lightning, rain, and mud—to Philadelphia so he could break the tie and cast Delaware's vote in favor of independence. Although seriously ill, Rodney then served the revolutionary cause as commander of Delaware's militia and as the state's governor.

FLORIDA

Nickname: Sunshine State | **Capital:** Tallahassee | **Statehood:** March 3, 1845 (27th)
Population: 15,111,244 (4th) | **Area:** 65,756 sq. mi. (22nd) | **Highest point:** 345 ft. (in Walton County)

A low-lying peninsula separating the Atlantic Ocean from the Gulf of Mexico, Florida also includes a narrow panhandle in the northwest. At the southern tip are the Keys, a chain of small islands that curve southwestward into the Caribbean Sea. Agriculture—especially citrus fruits and sugarcane—are important to Florida's economy, and its climate, scenery, and attractions draw millions of tourists seeking fun and sun. The Everglades and cypress swamps of southern Florida provide a refuge for wildlife, including panthers and crocodiles. Manatees (sea cows) lend their charms to warm coastal and inland waters.

Spanish explorer Juan Ponce de León's quest for the legendary Fountain of Youth brought him to Florida in 1513. Fort St. Augustine on the northeast coast is the oldest European settlement in the United States, founded in 1565. For the next two centuries, however, Florida lacked a strong European presence. In the early 1700s Seminole Indians from the Georgia-Alabama frontier settled the region. Following the American Revolution, American interests in Florida repeatedly conflicted with the Spanish and Indian presence. Although Spain ceded Florida to the United States following the First Seminole War (1817–1818), the Native American inhabitants resisted giving up their valuable land. Following the costly Second Seminole War (1835–1842), all but a few hundred Seminoles were removed to the territory of Oklahoma.

Since the late nineteenth century, Florida has experienced continuous growth. Because of the ongoing migration of retired people into the state, it has the nation's oldest population. Florida also has a strong international flavor. Over the last several decades, tides of new arrivals from Latin America—including thousands of Cubans who fled their island after Fidel Castro seized power in 1959—have changed the political and cultural character of the state. A gateway to the Southern Hemisphere, Miami has a culturally diverse population that speaks English and Spanish. Miami Beach is a top destination of international jetsetters, and its southern end is home to more than a dozen restored hotels that represent some of the best Art Deco architecture in the United States.

Disney

In the 1920s and 1930s movies provided patrons with a welcome escape from reality. American theatergoers especially relished Walt Disney's animated cartoons. His 1928 film, *Steamboat Willie*, starred Mickey Mouse, Disney's most popular and enduring character. Other animated Disney hits of the era include *Snow White and the Seven Dwarfs*, *Pinocchio*, and *Bambi*. In 1955 Disney opened an amusement park called Disneyland in Anaheim, California. Featuring historical reconstructions, futuristic displays, and thrill rides, it testified to the power of consumer culture in America. In 1971 a similar park, known as Walt Disney World Resort, opened near Orlando, Florida. By the 1990s Disney had become a leader of America's mass-culture industry. In addition to its theme parks, it makes popular animated and live-action movies, produces books and comic strips, and owns television networks and record companies.

Apollo 11

On July 16, 1969, Apollo 11—the first manned flight to the moon—lifted off from Florida's Kennedy Space Center. After a four-day trip, the astronauts arrived at the moon. When the Lunar Module "Eagle" carrying Neil Armstrong and Edwin "Buzz" Aldrin touched down on the relatively flat and unobstructed Sea of Tranquility site, it ushered in a new age of human exploration. The millions who watched on television as Armstrong took his first steps on the lunar surface were thrilled to hear him proclaim, "That's one small step for man, one giant leap for mankind." The product of a "space race" with the Soviet Union, the Apollo program ultimately included twelve manned missions between May 1961 and December 1972, six of which put men on the moon.

GEORGIA

Nickname: Empire State of the South | **Capital:** Atlanta | **Statehood:** January 2, 1788 (4th)
Population: 7,788,240 (10th) | **Area:** 59,441 sq. mi. (24th) | **Highest point:** 4,784 ft. (Brasstown Bald)

The largest state east of the Mississippi River, Georgia is generally flat. The middle part of the state, however, is characterized by rolling hills such as those around Stone Mountain. The Okefenokee Swamp, a vast watery region teeming with animal and plant life, covers Georgia's southeastern corner. While Georgia is the national leader in peanut production, it is also famous for its peaches. Its capital, Atlanta, has long been the principal city of the southeastern United States.

Founded in 1732, Georgia was the last of the thirteen original colonies to be settled. For the next hundred years, Georgians gradually forced the area's original inhabitants—the Creek and Cherokee Indians—to leave their lands. Because disease, starvation, and death accompanied these tribes on their journey westward, they labeled the journey the "Trail of Tears." The acquisition of Indian lands helped Georgia's vast cotton plantations flourish in the years leading up to the Civil War. Georgians not only grew cotton, they also turned it into cloth. Textile manufacturing is Georgia's oldest (and still largest) industry.

Georgia voted for secession in January 1861 and was a major source of supplies for the Confederacy. In the spring of 1864 a Union army commanded by General William T. Sherman invaded Georgia. After capturing Atlanta in September of that year, Sherman's troops continued their march to Savannah, leaving a path of devastation in their wake.

Following the war, Georgia, like other Southern states, imposed racial segregation and instituted poll taxes, literacy tests, and other devices to prevent blacks from voting. Reforms began in Georgia before other southern states, but many black Georgians were impatient with the slow pace of change and turned to activism. Led by Atlanta-born Martin Luther King Jr., these people fought on the frontlines of the civil rights movement.

Increasing numbers of black voters led to the election of African Americans to state and local offices. In 1972 Andrew Young became the state's first black congressman since Reconstruction. The next year, Maynard Jackson became Atlanta's first African-American mayor. Georgia's advances in the areas of politics, civil rights, and economic growth have made the state a symbol of the New South.

The Coca-Cola Company

In 1886 Atlanta pharmacist John Pemberton created a drink from carbonated water, sugar syrup, caffeine, and extracts of kola nuts and coca leaves. Named Coca-Cola after two of its ingredients, the beverage was one of the first U.S. products to benefit from a massive advertising campaign. Americans soon recognized Coca-Cola's logo and various slogans. In the twentieth century, the Coca-Cola Company continued to demonstrate a remarkable marketing ingenuity; it was the first company to use coupons to attract customers. During World War II, the company cultivated a taste for "Coke" among American troops. Expanding along with U.S. power and influence in the postwar period, Coca-Cola established a worldwide market. Today it is a truly global company, with bottling plants in more than sixty countries.

Cable News Network (CNN)

Founded in 1980 by businessman Ted Turner, and headquartered in Atlanta, CNN was the first 24-hour all-news network on television. During its first decade, CNN attracted viewers with its coverage of dramatic events such as the Space Shuttle *Challenger* explosion in 1986 and the fall of the Berlin Wall in 1989. CNN's round-the-clock coverage of the 1991 Persian Gulf War earned it international acclaim. During the conflict, the world watched with anxious fascination as the network broadcast live scenes of the aerial fireworks. Transmitted via satellite around the globe, the immediacy of CNN's reports has revolutionized the nature of news. Its coverage also influences the unfolding of events as they're being covered. Known as the "CNN effect," this phenomenon has intensified in recent years due to the proliferation of other 24-hour news channels.

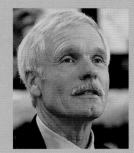

Ted Turner

HAWAII

Nickname: Aloha State | **Capital:** Honolulu | **Statehood:** August 21, 1959 (50th)
Population: 1,185,497 (42nd) | **Area:** 10,932 sq. mi. (43rd) | **Highest Point:** 13,796 ft. (Mauna Kea)

Composed of 124 islets and eight major islands—Niihau, Kauai, Hawaii, Oahu, Molokai, Lanai, Kahoolawe, and Maui—Hawaii covers more than 10,000 square miles. Hawaii's capital, Honolulu, holds most of the state's residents. Tourism is the state's strongest industry: during every season, millions of vacationers descend on Hawaii's luxurious beaches, crystal clear waters, and lively coral reefs. Cash crops like pineapples, sugarcane, and macadamia nuts also yield healthy profits, and the U.S. government supports the state by maintaining military installations on various islands.

Polynesians came to Hawaii in two waves: migrants from the Marquesas Islands arrived in the fifth century, and people from Tahiti landed roughly 500 years later. They lived in isolation until Captain James Cook of England "discovered" the islands in 1778. People from Asia, Europe, and North America soon began to settle the islands, bringing a host of deadly diseases with them. As a result, Hawaii's native population shrank by nearly 80 percent in less than a century.

Americans began to influence political developments on the islands almost immediately. When missionary William Richards came to Hawaii in 1822, he encouraged King Kamehameha III to issue a Declaration of Rights, an Edict of Toleration, and a formal constitution. The United States, Britain, and France responded by recognizing Hawaiian independence. Nevertheless, American businessmen controlled Hawaii's economy. During the first half of the twentieth century, five companies owned almost every sugarcane plantation. Because these businesses offered low pay and miserable working conditions, workers organized a union and, in 1946, went on strike. The strike's success advanced social justice and democracy on the Hawaiian Islands.

When Japan bombed the U.S. naval installation in Oahu's Pearl Harbor on December 7, 1941, Hawaii became a household word in mainland America. Though Hawaii was not yet a state, this Japanese action drew the United States into World War II. The memorial that now stands over the sunken battleship *Arizona* draws numerous tourists and preserves Hawaii's place in American memory.

Queen Liliuokalani (1838–1917)

The last Hawaiian monarch, Queen Liliuokalani devoted her life to preserving Hawaiian independence. When she took the throne in 1891, the queen attempted to reduce the power of American businessmen and hinder the U.S. government's attempt to annex Hawaii. Tensions between Americans and Hawaiians increased during the next two years and, when Liluokalani attempted to draft a new constitution for the islands in January 1893, Americans removed her from power and abolished the Hawaiian monarchy. When the former queen died in 1917, she became a symbol of Hawaiian independence. A statue of her now stands in the city of Honolulu.

Pearl Harbor

Located on the Hawaiian Island of Oahu, Pearl Harbor houses America's Pacific Fleet. It became a national landmark when Japanese planes unexpectedly attacked it on December 7, 1941. Because America's aircraft carriers were on maneuvers during the attack, the Japanese did not sink the most important parts of the U.S. Navy. By 1943 America had rebounded from the losses it suffered at Pearl Harbor (several battleships and thousands of people) and taken command of the war against Japan. Nevertheless, Pearl Harbor is a place seared into national memory. A memorial currently rests over the sunken hull of the battleship Arizona, allowing tourists to peer down at the vessel and contemplate the horrors of war.

IDAHO

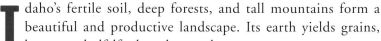

Nickname: Gem State | **Capital:** Boise | **Statehood:** July 3, 1890 (43rd)
Population: 1,251,700 (40th) | **Area:** 83,574 sq. mi. (14th) | **Highest point:** 12,662 ft. (Borah Peak)

Idaho's fertile soil, deep forests, and tall mountains form a beautiful and productive landscape. Its earth yields grains, beans, and alfalfa, but the state's most famous crop is the potato. Ranchers tend cattle and sheep along Idaho's prairies, and loggers convert commercial woodlands into high-grade lumber. Miners also contribute to Idaho's economy, taking lead and silver from the ground. In recent years, manufacturing has come to the state. Industrial plants process foodstuffs, forest goods, and mined materials into marketable products.

When the Lewis and Clark expedition arrived in Idaho in 1805, it encountered many Indian peoples, including the Kalispel, Nez Perce, and Shoshoni. Traders and missionaries followed, but the white population remained small until prospectors discovered gold in 1860. Businessmen, miners, and loggers then stormed into Idaho, seeking their fortunes. Their conflicting points of view soon collided, however, and state politics grew more volatile as time passed. Idaho

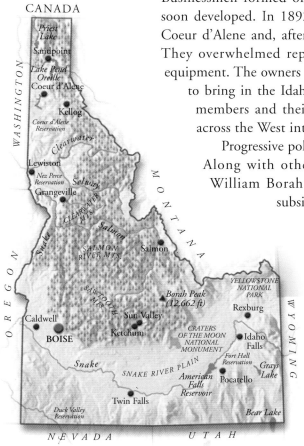

workers rebelled against long workdays and harsh working conditions, joining radical labor unions like the Western Federation of Miners and the International Workers of the World. Businessmen formed organizations of their own, and conflicts soon developed. In 1892 miners declared a strike in the city of Coeur d'Alene and, after growing frustrated, attacked the mines. They overwhelmed replacement workers and seized valuable equipment. The owners responded by convincing the government to bring in the Idaho National Guard, which arrested union members and their sympathizers. Such conflicts occurred across the West into the early twentieth century.

Progressive politics grew in Idaho as the state developed. Along with other Western politicians, Idaho Senator William Borah persuaded the central government to subsidize his region's development during the 1930s. In doing so, he helped cement Washington, D.C.'s influence on Western life.

Gifted with striking geographical features, Idaho showcases the outdoor life. Skiers flock to Sun Valley, campers visit Yellowstone National Park, and the Snake River carries rafters across the southern and western portions of the state. Hells Canyon—North America's deepest gorge—is one of the most stunning sights in the United States.

The Lost Generation

Following World War I, a number of American writers—including Ernest Hemingway, John Dos Passos, F. Scott Fitzgerald, and e.e. cummings—wrote novels and poems that expressed discontent with postwar life. Although many Americans remembered World War I fondly and valued the mass culture that developed during the 1920s, these writers disagreed and spent a number of years in self-imposed exile. They became collectively known as the "Lost Generation" when another American writer, Gertrude Stein, referred to them in this way. Hemingway best represented this group's alienation by publishing *The Sun Also Rises* in 1926. When he died in Ketcham, Idaho, more than thirty years later, Hemingway still stood for the Lost Generation.

Ernest Hemingway

William E. Borah (1865–1940)

A lifelong politician, William Borah represented Idaho in the U.S. Senate for thirty-three years. Elected to the Senate in 1906, he won fame after the First World War by opposing President Woodrow Wilson's attempt to place the United States in an international collective security system known as the League of Nations. Although many people considered Borah an "isolationist"—someone opposed to American activity abroad—Borah believed the United States could play an important role in international affairs. During the 1930s, for example, Borah encouraged President Franklin Roosevelt to improve relations with Latin American nations by supporting FDR's Good Neighbor Policy. At home, he backed FDR's New Deal, arguing that the federal government should help develop the American West.

ILLINOIS

Nickname: Prairie State | **Capital:** Springfield | **Statehood:** December 3, 1818 (21st)
Population: 12,128,370 (5th) | **Area:** 57,918 sq. mi. (25th) | **Highest point:** 1,235 ft. (Charles Mound)

Named after an Indian tribe, Illinois maintains a culturally diverse population. African Americans, ethnic whites, and other groups work in a variety of fields, especially agriculture and industry. Benefiting from rich coal and oil deposits, the state exports fossil fuels across the nation. Fertile soil covers most of the region, allowing farmers to produce mass quantities of soybeans and grains. Some farmers raise cattle and hogs, selling their meat and dairy products. Illinois' largest city, Chicago, accommodates a heavy concentration of factories that produce fabricated metals, processed foods, rubber products, and electrical equipment. Publishing houses also prosper in Illinois, giving the state a worldly flavor.

Native-American populations—including the Illinois, Kickapoo, Chippewa, and Peoria tribes—thrived in the region for centuries. But their landholdings decreased after the Europeans arrived. French explorers made inroads in Illinois during the seventeenth century, and Great Britain controlled the territory after 1763. The United States claimed Illinois following the

American Revolution, and settlers inundated the region throughout the nineteenth century.

The state benefited from the Industrial Revolution, as available factory work drew European immigrants to Chicago. Because industries offered dangerous working conditions and low pay, many laborers adopted radical politics, demanding higher wages and safer workplaces. When management refused to meet their demands, violence erupted. On May 4, 1886, militants gathered in Chicago's Haymarket Square to protest workers' plight. After nearly 200 police officers tried to suppress them, a bomb exploded, killing seven officers and wounding several others. Fearing that labor violence would spread, President Grover Cleveland used army troops, professional strikebreakers, and local police to quash future strikes and protests.

The state's diverse populace has produced both benefits and problems. Although a multi-ethnic labor force has fueled economic growth for more than a century, whites and blacks often have come into conflict. Still, the civil rights movement of the 1950s and 1960s enhanced interracial cooperation in Illinois. Race relations are now better than ever.

The 1968 Democratic National Convention

In August 1968 thousands of Americans—most of them young people—gathered at Chicago's Democratic Convention to denounce the Vietnam War. Convinced that the government had to withdraw U.S. troops from Southeast Asia, protestors gathered in Grant Park, Lincoln Park, and other areas to make their feelings known. When the Democrats endorsed an aggressive Vietnam policy, the protesters chanted anti-government slogans and displayed subversive banners. The Chicago Police overreacted and pummeled the protestors with fists and nightsticks. Although most journalists reacted with horror, the majority of Americans endorsed the police violence, indicating that they had tired of protest politics. America would not remove its troops until 1974, after tens of thousands more Americans lost their lives.

Immigration

Between 1885 and 1917, nearly eighteen million immigrants from Central and Southeastern Europe moved into large industrial cities like Chicago. Although many of these immigrants could not speak English, they found work in America's numerous factories and helped make the United States a powerful and prosperous nation. Because they often received low wages for hard work, many of these immigrants joined labor unions, making organizations like the American Federation of Labor and the Congress of Industrial Workers stronger than ever before. Chicago reformer Jane Addams also tried to help the city's immigrant population by opening Hull House in 1889. Addams and her staff offered suffering immigrants hot meals, health care, and educational programs, making the city more hospitable as a result.

Children at Hull House

INDIANA

Nickname: Hoosier State | **Capital:** Indianapolis | **Statehood:** December 11, 1816 (19th)
Population: 5,942,901 (14th) | **Area:** 36,420 sq. mi. (38th) | **Highest point:** 1,257 ft. (in Franklin Township)

Thought to mean "land of the Indians," Indiana possesses rich soil, along with deposits of sand, gravel, and coal. The central and northern portions of the state are home to large farms and truck gardens (vegetable farms), while southern Indiana favors woodlands and limestone quarries. Industry also flourishes in Indiana. Workers in the city of Elkhart produce musical instruments, and laborers in Fort Wayne manufacture tools used in diamond mining. Although the state capital of Indianapolis is modeled after the cosmopolitan cities of Washington, D.C. and Versailles, France, Indiana is known for its numerous small cities and towns.

Before Europeans first traveled to Indiana, Native American peoples including the Miami, Piankashaw, and Wea populated the area. Great Britain, however, won control of the land following the French and Indian War in 1763. The British then lost the region in the American Revolution, and the United States government made Indiana part of its vast Northwest Territory after 1783. When southern settlers brought

slaves to the region, Indiana politics changed remarkably. The area took on a southern flavor, and its largely white population endeavored to maintain firm control over African Americans and other minorities—a desire that was often revealed through acts of bigotry. During the early twentieth century, the hate group Ku Klux Klan (KKK) flowered in Indiana. Although the Indiana KKK discriminated against African Americans, it also aimed its hate at Jews, Catholics, and immigrants. Ironically, left-wing politics also had blossomed in Indiana. Dissident politician Eugene V. Debs served in the Indiana legislature in 1885 and became president of the American Railway Union eight years later. Using the state as a launching pad, Debs later ran for president five times. Although he never won, Debs collected an impressive 915,000 votes in 1920.

When many people think of Indiana, they think of the typical Indianan: the Hoosier. Blessed with small-town charm and homespun wisdom, Hoosiers evoke a time in American history when life was thought to be simple and good. They symbolize enduring American values.

Progressive Imperialism

During the last years of the nineteenth century, the United States began to assert its power abroad. Advocates of national expansion argued that America could serve the interests of itself and foreign peoples at the same time. Indiana Senator Albert Beveridge became one of the most vocal supporters of progressive imperialism, reminding people in speeches like "The March of the Flag" that an American empire promised to generate progress throughout the world. Although Beveridge understood that residents of the Philippines, Hawaii, and Cuba would resist American expansion, he insisted that exposure to American morals, values, and politics would benefit them in the long run. Popular with many Americans, Beveridge's ideas helped make the United States one of the world's great powers.

Senator Albert Beveridge

Sports Culture

Sport has become very important in the contemporary United States. Many Americans are drawn to the spectacle of competition, and show their fondness for sport by clothing themselves in athlete-endorsed apparel and annually purchasing millions of dollars worth of memorabilia. Residents of Indiana have displayed a particular appreciation for basketball. The 1987 film *Hoosiers* suggested that the state's residents make high-school basketball an important part of civic life, and the Indiana University basketball team receives similar attention. Indeed, sport has rooted itself across the globe. Capitalism and the values it encompasses have become closely linked to the popularity of sports.

IOWA

Nickname: Hawkeye State | **Capital:** Des Moines | **Statehood:** December 28, 1846 (29th)
Population: 2,969,413 (30th) | **Area:** 56,276 sq. mi. (26th) | **Highest point:** 1,670 ft. (Ocheyedan Mound)

Named after an Indian tribe, Iowa is a land of famously fertile soil. Iowa farmers produce a huge harvest of cash crops each year, and keep valuable stocks of cattle and hogs. Ironically, farmers are often too productive. In the past, they have produced more food than Americans could consume, creating a surplus that has driven crop prices down and limited their profits.

Spaniards traveled to the region in the eighteenth century to mine rich lead deposits. Americans secured portions of Iowa with the Louisiana Purchase of 1803 and, some thirty years later, purchased the rest of the state's land from the Saulk and Fox Indians. Iowa's population steadily increased as Americans arrived to take advantage of the state's fertile soil. In the years before the Civil War, some residents became part of the Underground Railroad, a system in which opponents of slavery provided safe havens for slaves fleeing their southern masters. When the Civil War finally erupted in 1861, the state provided the Union Army with an impressive number of soldiers.

After the Civil War, settlers teemed into Iowa. America's new railroad system provided them with opportunities to ship crops to market, and a decline in Indian power convinced people they could farm in peace. Religious communities joined the migration to Iowa. The Amana Colony—a Christian group dedicated to communal living—moved to the state in 1855, and Protestant sects like the Quakers and the Amish also established a presence in Iowa. Their collective belief in a strict moral code gave Iowa politics a decidedly conservative flavor. Indeed, one of America's most conservative presidents, Herbert Hoover, was born to a Quaker family in West Branch, Iowa.

In W. P. Kinsella's 1982 book *Shoeless Joe*, the author speaks of Iowa's soil in hallowed terms—it is as rich as "chocolate pudding," the stuff of dreams. Most importantly, the soil provides Iowans with their livelihood. Indeed Iowa's many farms help make America "bread basket" to the world. When necessary, the United States can ship abundant supplies of food across the globe and feed hungry people. For these men, women, and children, Iowa means hope.

The Amana Colony

Formed in Germany in the eighteenth century, the Amana Colony was a community of Christian believers that sought a personal relationship with God through rigorous bible study and humble prayer. According to founding members, mainstream churches overemphasized formal rituals and intellectual debates: they had lost the real meaning of God's will. In 1842 roughly 350 community members came to America and purchased a 5,000-acre site in Buffalo, New York. When its membership topped 1,200 in 1855, the community moved to Iowa because the state offered large tracts of land for reasonable prices. In 1932 the Amana Colony incorporated as the Amana Society and began to produce commodities like refrigerators, freezers, and washing machines that sold for impressive profits. Even today, the Amana Society continues to flourish.

Herbert C. Hoover (1874–1964)

Born in West Branch, Iowa, Herbert Hoover was orphaned at the age of nine and grew up with his uncle in Oregon. After attending Stanford University, he became a strong advocate of public service. He helped evacuate Americans trapped in Europe when World War I erupted in 1914, and later led America's effort to ration and distribute food during the war. Elected president as a Republican in 1928, Hoover faced a series of problems. The stock market crash of October 1929 and the ensuing Great Depression proved to be challenges he could not overcome, and people resented his failure to help them. Hoover lost his bid for reelection in 1932 but remained a respected figure for the rest of his life.

KANSAS

Nickname: Sunflower State | **Capital:** Topeka | **Statehood:** January 29, 1861 (34th)
Population: 2,654,052 (32nd) | **Area:** 82,282 sq. mi. (15th) | **Highest point:** 4,039 ft. (Mount Sunflower)

Named after the Kansa—or Kaw—Indians, Kansas marks the geographic center of the continental United States. Although most people consider it a uniformly flat landmass, the state is actually geographically diverse. Chalk spires and shallow gullies appear throughout western Kansas, and its northeastern section contains timbered hills and gushing springs. Because the state once stood at the base of an inland sea, it has incredibly fertile soil. Much of America's wheat comes from Kansas, and its abundant grass fields allow cattle ranchers to prosper. Industry also flourishes in the state. Wichita, one of its biggest cities, produces enough aircraft to be known as the "Air Capital of the World."

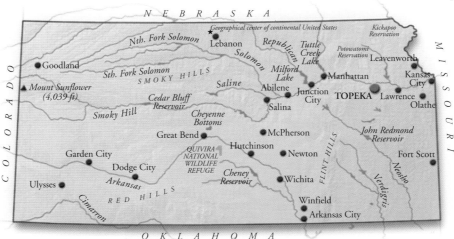

Long before European settlers arrived in Kansas, Indian peoples developed agricultural communities along the state's Republican and Big Blue rivers. Spanish explorers arrived during the sixteenth century, and French fur traders moved into the region nearly one hundred years later. The United States secured the region in the Louisiana Purchase of 1803, designated it Indian Territory, and allowed displaced tribes to settle there. As the nation sped toward civil war during the 1850s, Kansas became a seedbed for sectional tensions and border violence. Because the Kansas-Nebraska Act of 1854 allowed state residents to decide whether or not they would legalize slavery, proslavery and antislavery activists repeatedly clashed. Violence in the region exploded, causing people to name the area "Bleeding Kansas."

Although the state is home to people of all faiths, Kansas possesses a striking number of Protestant sects. Worshipping along with Methodists, Baptists, and Lutherans are rare groups like the Amish, Dunkard Brethren, and River Brethren. In fact, the state's most accomplished son, Republican President Dwight D. Eisenhower, grew up in a River Brethren household. As president, Eisenhower spread heartland values across the United States. He never forgot his Kansas roots, reminding Americans that national progress required them to work hard, make sacrifices, and help their neighbors.

Bleeding Kansas

Following the passage of the Kansas-Nebraska Act in 1854, legions of supporters and opponents of slavery flooded into Kansas in an effort to strengthen their respective causes. Because Missouri and Kansas shared a border, many slave-owning Missouri residents believed escaped slaves would use Kansas as a safe haven. In the end, both sides of the slavery debate used force to defend their ideas. During the mid-1850s, proslavery Border Ruffians from Missouri crossed into Kansas, burning homes and destroying businesses. Abolitionists led by John Brown responded in kind, killing several proslavery activists near Potawatomie Creek. In many respects, events in Kansas served as a rehearsal for the Civil War.

Dwight David Eisenhower (1890–1969)

The thirty-fourth president of the United States, Eisenhower—"Ike" to his friends—grew up in Abilene, Kansas. He was a member of a poor family and decided to attend the U.S. Military Academy at West Point in 1911 because he wanted a free education. As a soldier, Eisenhower steadily advanced in

Dwight D. Eisenhower (center left)

rank and earned glory in World War II by commanding Allied forces in Europe. After leading his troops to victory, he became the president of Columbia University and, later, the first commander of the North American Treaty Organization (NATO). He won landslide victories in the presidential elections of 1952 and 1956 and remained popular with millions of Americans before dying in 1969. He is buried in Abilene, not far from his childhood home.

KENTUCKY

Nickname: Bluegrass State | **Capital:** Frankfort | **Statehood:** June 1, 1792 (15th)
Population: 3,960, 825 (25th) | **Area:** 40,411 sq. mi. (37th) | **Highest point:** 4,139 ft. (Black Mountain)

Located on the border between North and South, Kentucky's boundaries are formed on three sides by rivers. Its landscape ranges from the Cumberland region's heavily forested ridges and narrow valleys to the gently rolling hills and knobby crests of the Bluegrass region (the grass in this region has a bluish tint when seen from a distance). A state of small towns and rural crossroads, much of American folk music comes from Kentucky. The state is among the nation's leaders in coal production, and accounts for about one-quarter of America's tobacco crop.

Kentucky was the home of various Indian tribes when Daniel Boone and other frontiersmen settled it in the early 1770s. In 1775 Boone blazed a trail westward through the Cumberland Gap. Boone's trail later formed a leg of the famous Wilderness Road. Although Native Americans vigorously defended their lands against white encroachment, thousands of settlers migrated to this frontier region following the American Revolution.

Throughout the first half the nineteenth century, Kentucky, like other slaveholding border states, favored compromise between North and South. Kentuckian Henry Clay engineered the Missouri Compromise of 1820 and the Compromise of 1850, both of which addressed the extension of slavery into new territories. Throughout the Civil War, Kentucky residents remained divided in their loyalties: about 100,000 joined the Union Army and 40,000 fought for the Confederacy. Because both the Union and the Confederacy claimed the state, Kentucky was at the mercy of occupying armies and suffered numerous guerrilla raids.

Kentucky recovered from the war better than many Southern states, but prosperous economic times did not last. Kentuckians were involved in the populist agrarian politics of the late nineteenth century, and participated in the 1930s labor unrest known as the "Coal Wars." In the 1960s Kentucky was one of the main targets of President Lyndon Johnson's "War on Poverty." Since that time, Kentucky's economic fortunes have steadily improved. Along with whiskey, Kentucky is best known for breeding Thoroughbred horses. The Kentucky Derby, held since 1875 at Louisville's Churchill Downs on the first Saturday of May each year, is the first leg of the Triple Crown of American Thoroughbred racing.

Abraham Lincoln (1809–1865)

The son of a Kentucky frontiersman, Abraham Lincoln had a humble backwoods childhood. Despite having less than a year of formal education, he became a successful lawyer and politician in Illinois. In 1860 Lincoln ran for president as an antislavery Republican. His victory caused several southern states to secede from the Union, precipitating the Civil War. Throughout the bloody four-year fight, Lincoln proved a decisive and capable leader. He became a symbol of the Union, and his words and actions—such as the Emancipation Proclamation and the Gettysburg Address—gave eloquent purpose to the conflict. On April 14, 1865, only five days after the Confederate surrender, Lincoln was assassinated by John Wilkes Booth, a southern sympathizer. Millions of Americans mourned the passing of the president who had redefined the nation.

Abraham Lincoln (right)

Jefferson Davis (1808–1889)

The capture of Jefferson Davis

Born in Kentucky, Jefferson Davis was the first and only president of the Confederate States of America. Throughout his career—which included stints as a soldier, a senator from Mississippi, and secretary of war—Davis consistently supported slavery and states' rights. As president of the Confederacy, he faced enormous problems. The new nation had to create everything from a constitution to postage stamps. Some of the actions Davis took to fight the war—such as drafting soldiers—conflicted with the southern belief in states' rights, and many governors refused to cooperate with his administration. A month after the Confederacy collapsed, federal troops captured Davis, who had fled the Confederate capital of Richmond, Virginia. Released from prison in 1868, Davis spent the rest of his life engaged in a number of unsuccessful business ventures.

LOUISIANA

Nickname: Pelican State | **Capital:** Baton Rouge | **Statehood:** April 30, 1812 (18th)
Population: 4,375,035 (22nd) | **Area:** 51,843 sq. mi. (31st) | **Highest point:** 535 ft. (Driskill Mountain)

Located where the waters of the great Mississippi River system flow into the Gulf of Mexico, Louisiana is a rich agricultural region. The lush vegetation of its shores and bayous conceal a wealth of natural gas and oil, causing the state to be among the nation's leaders in petroleum production. Since 1682, when France first claimed the region, several flags have flown over Louisiana. The resulting variety of traditions and cultures continue to color the social and political life of the state.

The United States acquired most of Louisiana in 1803 as part of the Louisiana Purchase. On January 8, 1815, American forces commanded by Andrew Jackson defeated the British at the Battle of New Orleans. The decisive victory, though won after the signing of the Treaty of Ghent, solidified the young republic's independence. After the War of 1812, settlers streamed into Louisiana. Sugarcane and cotton plantations flourished, and New Orleans became a leading commercial center. Although the state was detached from most Civil War fighting, Union forces occupied New Orleans in May 1862 and placed the city under martial law.

Throughout the late nineteenth and early twentieth centuries, poverty was widespread among Louisiana's rural population. Cotton prices declined sharply following World War I and remained at low levels throughout the 1920s. Hard times and general discontent enabled the rise of politician Huey P. Long. Freewheeling and colorful, Long—elected governor in 1928 and senator in 1930—championed the interests of small farmers and laborers against those of powerful corporations. Although he was assassinated in 1935, Long's family continued to control Louisiana politics for several decades after his death.

The Louisiana French peoples—called "Cajuns"—continue to influence much of southern Louisiana society. Similarly, the "Creoles" (descendants of French and Spanish settlers) have developed a distinctive culture and cuisine centered in New Orleans. That city is also the birthplace of American jazz music and hosts the annual Mardi Gras celebration marked by parades featuring spectacular floats, masked balls, dancing in the streets, and indulgence in food and drink.

Jazz

In the early twentieth century a new type of music bubbled up in New Orleans. Blending African, American, and European musical traditions with free-flowing melodies and improvised rhythms, performers like Jelly Roll Morton, King Oliver, and Louis Armstrong created a distinctively American sound. In the 1920s groups like the Original Dixieland Jazz Band, the New Orleans Rhythm Kings, and the Creole Jazz Band created a national sensation. Many New Orleans musicians migrated to other cities like Chicago, Memphis, Kansas City, and New York, where they stimulated the evolution of new styles. Since its beginnings, jazz has undergone several periods of experimentation and development. Innovators like Duke Ellington, Count Basie, Charlie Parker, and Miles Davis furthered both the popularity of jazz and its development as a serious art form.

Mahalia Jackson

French Exploration of North America

In 1682 the French explorer Rene-Robert de La Salle traveled down the Mississippi River to the Gulf of Mexico and claimed for France all the land drained by the river and its tributaries. La Salle named the vast region Louisiana in honor of the reigning French king, Louis XIV. In 1718 the French built a fort at New Orleans to secure the area against France's rival colonial powers, Spain and Great Britain. Attempts by the French to settle Louisiana largely failed, however, and several decades of warfare drained their strength in the region. In 1762 France decided that Louisiana was not worth the expense and transferred it to Spain. Thirty-eight years later, Spain gave the region back to France. France, in turn, sold it to the United States in 1803.

MAINE

Nickname: Pine Tree State | **Capital:** Augusta | **Statehood:** March 15, 1820 (23rd)
Population: 1,253,040 (39th) | **Area:** 35,387 sq. mi. (39th) | **Highest point:** 5,267 ft. (Mount Katahdin)

Lying at the northeastern tip of the country, Maine is the least populated state east of the Mississippi River. The Appalachian Mountains extend into Maine, creating a rugged inland terrain and producing a rich supply of lumber. Maine's famed rocky coastline—totaling some 3,500 miles and indented with numerous natural harbors—provides a home for most of the state's residents and facilitates its important fishing and tourist industries.

In the sixteenth century Portuguese, Spanish, French, and English explorers began to probe the bays, coves, and inlets of Maine, establishing fisheries on some of the coastal islands and trading fur with the Algonquin Indians. Throughout the seventeenth and eighteenth centuries, Maine attracted a substantial number of Scotch-Irish Protestant immigrants hoping to make their fortune by exploiting the state's abundant supply of furs, fish, and forests. Entering the Union as a free state under the Missouri Compromise of 1820, Maine provided a home for the pre-Civil War abolitionist movement. Maine residents were also prominent in later reform movements such as prohibition and women's suffrage. Moreover, Maine's Margaret Chase Smith became the first woman to serve in both houses of Congress when she was elected to the U.S. Senate in 1948. Her 1950 speech, "Declaration of Conscience"—which criticized the excesses of America's anticommunist position—honored Maine's tradition of principled dissent. Today Maine is one of only three states with two female senators. It has also led the way on enviornmental issues. Many of Maine's environmental laws serve as national models.

Maine's many lakes, rivers, woodlands, and mountains have made the state a popular summer playground. Its scenic beauty has also made it a haven for writers and artists. People from across the United States have long appreciated the literary work of Henry Wadsworth Longfellow and the paintings of Winslow Homer and Edward Hopper. The writer most identified with Maine is Stephen King. A native of the state, many of his novels of horror and suspense are set there.

Colonial Conflicts

From the late seventeenth century to the mid-eighteenth century, English settlers fought a series of wars against Native Americans and their French allies throughout New England. The principal cause of these clashes was English settlement on native lands, although local tribes also had specific grievances against the settlers. These conflicts—such as King Philip's War (1675–1678) and Queen Anne's War (1702–1713)—devastated towns throughout the region, inflicted numerous human casualties, and left a legacy of bitterness on both sides. The 1763 Treaty of Paris, which ended the French and Indian War, also marked the end of Native American resistance in the area. Maine's Penobscot and Passamaquoddy tribes were moved to reservations, while other native groups moved to join Abenaki villages in Canada.

Joshua Chamberlain and the 20th Maine Regiment

In the summer of 1863 General Robert E. Lee led the Confederate Army of Northern Virginia across the Potomac River into Maryland and southern Pennsylvania. At Gettysburg, Pennsylvania, on a hot and humid July 1, Lee confronted Union forces led by General George G. Meade. On the third day of fighting, Lee sent his men forward in a desperate attack on the fortified Union positions. Defending a rocky, wooded slope called "Little Round Top," Colonel Joshua L. Chamberlain's 20th Maine Regiment achieved lasting fame by repelling repeated Confederate assaults. The Union victory at Gettysburg was a turning point in the war. Nearly two years later, Chamberlain—who won a medal of honor for his actions at Gettysburg—supervised the Confederate surrender ceremony.

Joshua Chamberlain

MARYLAND

Nickname: Old Line State | **Capital:** Annapolis | **Statehood:** April 28, 1788 (7th)
Population: 5,171,634 (19th) | **Area:** 12,407 sq. mi. (42nd) | **Highest point:** 3,360 ft. (Backbone Mountain)

Maryland's diverse landscape includes the marshy Eastern Shore, the metropolitan bustle of Baltimore, and the forested Appalachian foothills. The Chesapeake Bay has one of the world's richest concentrations of marine life, including a famous and profitable population of blue crabs. Maryland's northern border with Pennsylvania marks the famous Mason-Dixon Line, drawn in the 1760s and traditionally regarded as the boundary between the North and the South.

Founded as a haven for Roman Catholics escaping England's religious restrictions, Maryland and its residents were deeply involved in the events surrounding the American struggle for independence. Maryland also played a key role in the early development of the new republic. After witnessing the futile British bombardment of Fort McHenry in Baltimore Harbor during the War of 1812, Francis Scott Key wrote the "Star-Spangled Banner," which later became America's national anthem.

Although it was a slaveholding state, Maryland remained loyal to the Union during the Civil War. Several clashes between Union and Confederate troops occurred on its soil, including the Battle of Antietam, the war's single bloodiest day. The Union victory there on September 1, 1862, encouraged President Abraham Lincoln to announce the Emancipation Proclamation. The Proclamation became law on January 1, 1863, effectively freeing all slaves in rebel states and territories. After the Civil War, blacks found Maryland more congenial than the states of the former Confederacy. Baltimore in particular was home to a vibrant black community and boasts the second-oldest chapter of the National Association for the Advancement of Colored People (NAACP). Following World War II, Marylanders remained active in the movement for racial justice and civil rights. Baltimore attorney Thurgood Marshall led the successful legal challenge to racial segregation in schools. Later, Marshall sat on the Supreme Court as its first African-American member, serving from 1967 to 1991.

In 1790 Maryland ceded land along the Potomac River for the site of a permanent federal capital, called the "District of Columbia." Now known as Washington, D.C., it has had a profound effect on Maryland's economic and cultural development, especially in towns like Bethesda and Silver Spring.

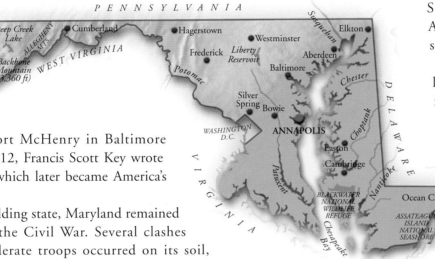

H.L. Mencken (1880–1956)

Born in Baltimore, Henry Louis Mencken was one of the most influential writers of the 1920s and 1930s. In 1899 Mencken began his journalism career with the *Baltimore Morning Herald*. In 1906 he switched to the *Baltimore Sun*, where he remained in various editorial capacities for most of his life. Mencken also edited several magazines, including the *Smart Set* and *American Mercury*. The primary targets of Mencken's perceptive, witty, and merciless criticisms were the shortcomings of American democracy and the foibles of middle-class culture. A fierce foe of governmental attacks on individual liberty, Mencken's characteristic style and controversial substance influenced many writers who followed him.

Maryland Abolitionists

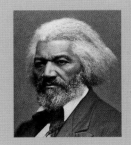
Frederick Douglass

Born a slave on a Maryland plantation, Frederick Douglass learned to read and write from his master's wife. After escaping from his plantation, he traveled to Massachusetts, where he became a vocal and eloquent opponent of slavery. By 1848 Douglass had established an abolitionist newspaper called the *North Star*. When he published his autobiography—*My Bondage, My Freedom*—in 1855, Douglass became the most respected African-American abolitionist in the United States. Harriet Tubman—born into slavery three years after Douglass on a different Maryland plantation—escaped from her master in 1848. For the next twelve years, Tubman was a prominent member of the Underground Railroad, an informal system by which black and white Americans helped escaped slaves move toward safety in the North. She helped an estimated 300 slaves gain freedom before the Civil War.

MASSACHUSETTS

Nickname: Bay State | **Capital:** Boston | **Statehood:** February 6, 1788 (6th)
Population: 6,175,169 (13th) | **Area:** 10,555 sq. mi. (44th) | **Highest Point:** 3,487 ft. (Mount Greylock)

Massachusetts's jagged 1,500-mile coastline winds in and out of scenic harbors and around small islands. In the southeast, Cape Cod, a 65-mile long appendage, juts out into the ocean to create the state's most identifiable physical feature. Its offshore waters are among the most treacherous in the country for fishermen and seagoing vessels. Also off the southeastern coast lie the islands of Nantucket and Martha's Vineyard, lashed by the Atlantic Ocean in winter but alive with tourists and seasonal residents during the summer.

Like many of the original thirteen colonies, Massachusetts was founded by people seeking a new way of life. The Pilgrims, who arrived in Massachusetts aboard the Mayflower in 1620, fled England to practice their religion freely. Having established their "city upon a hill," however, these Puritan settlers did not practice religious tolerance, persecuting and banishing groups with differing religious views. Nevertheless, the Puritans established an influential form of democratic self-governance, and Massachusetts provided both the ideological principles and many of the leaders of the American Revolution. Events in and near Boston—such as the Boston Massacre, the Boston Tea Party and, the Battles of Lexington and Concord—typified the spirit of independence that unified the colonies.

Throughout the nineteenth century, Massachusetts relied upon a diversified economy. Fishing was lucrative but dangerous, especially at the height of the whaling boom. Shipbuilding and maritime commerce further reinforced Massachusetts's ties to the sea. Led by Francis Cabot Lowell's mechanized textile factory, the state spearheaded the Industrial Revolution. Among the long-term consequences of the shift from agriculture to a manufacturing economy were increased urbanization and a large population of low-paid immigrant workers, who tended to support liberal politics.

From its beginnings, Massachusetts has played an important role in national politics. It has contributed several presidents—John Adams, John Quincy Adams, and John F. Kennedy—as well as other key statesmen and congressional leaders. It is also a cultural and intellectual center, sustaining several prominent universities and counting Ralph Waldo Emerson, Henry David Thoreau, Nathaniel Hawthorne, Louisa May Alcott, Emily Dickinson, and W.E.B. Du Bois among its great writers and thinkers.

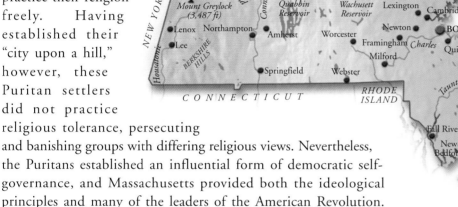

Margaret Fuller (1810–1850)

A groundbreaking writer and thinker, Margaret Fuller was one of the nineteenth century's most influential women. She worked with fellow Massachusetts residents Ralph Waldo Emerson, Henry David Thoreau, and Bronson Alcott to develop and describe Transcendentalism, a philosophy that values self-reliance, individualism, intuition, and the natural world. Fuller wrote for and edited a Transcendentalist journal, *The Dial*, and in 1845 she published *Women in the Nineteenth Century*. Her book called for more women's rights and, three years later, inspired the formation of the Seneca Falls Convention to support the cause. Fuller later became the first female news correspondent when she traveled to Italy to report on the European revolutions of 1848.

W.E.B. Du Bois (1868–1963)

Massachusetts native William Edward Burghardt Du Bois was the most influential African-American intellectual of his time. Du Bois attended Fisk University in Nashville, where he first experienced southern racial restrictions such as segregation. After becoming the first black to receive a Ph.D. from Harvard, Du Bois harshly criticized fellow African-American leader Booker T. Washington's strategy of accommodation and compromise with whites. His research into the social and economic conditions of black Americans convinced him that they needed to challenge segregation and discrimination through political action and higher education. A founding member of the NAACP, Du Bois edited its journal, *The Crisis*, which became a powerful voice for black civil rights. Active in the fight against racial discrimination until his death, Du Bois also left a distinguished record as a scholar and author.

MICHIGAN

Nickname: Wolverine State | **Capital:** Lansing | **Statehood:** January 26, 1837 (26th)
Population: 9,863,775 (8th) | **Area:** 96, 705 sq. mi. (11th) | **Highest point:** 1,979 ft. (Mount Arvon)

Split into two peninsulas by the Great Lakes, Michigan's unique landscape is home to a diverse economy. The Upper Peninsula possesses rich deposits of copper and iron ores that miners have exploited for generations. Tourists also enjoy the region in great numbers, hunting and fishing along the area's plentiful rivers and beaches. The Lower Peninsula, in contrast, features fertile soil that farmers use to grow potatoes and grains. But it is the automotive industry that represents the heart of Michigan's economy. In the early twentieth century, the city of Detroit began to produce automobiles and, although foreign competition has limited profits in recent years, Michigan continues to employ thousands of automotive workers and to build a majority of America's domestic automobile fleet.

French trappers and missionaries first came to the area in the seventeenth century, hoping to develop a fur trade and convert Native Americans to Christianity. Following a long military conflict with France, Great Britain won control of the region in 1763. Michigan became part of the United States following the American Revolution, and its population increased as new modes of transportation, such as steamships, opened the state for development.

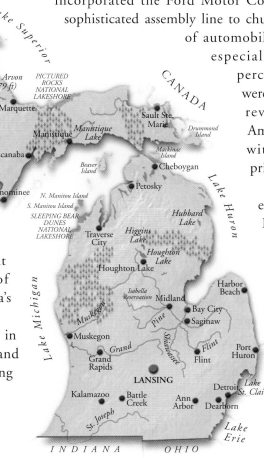

The production of cars became central to Michigan life during the early twentieth century. Entrepreneur Henry Ford incorporated the Ford Motor Company in 1903 and used a sophisticated assembly line to churn out a remarkable number of automobiles. Ford's Model T became especially popular: by 1918, 50 percent of the cars in America were Model Ts. These cars had a revolutionary influence on American life, providing people with unprecedented levels of privacy and mobility.

Racial tensions accompanied economic growth in Michigan. During World War II, African Americans moved to the state in large numbers and took factory jobs. Tensions mounted, producing severe riots in 1943 and 1967. Hard feelings linger, but Michigan remains a congenial place. The state annually draws numerous tourists eager to hike, hunt, fish, and sail in Michigan's great outdoors.

Motown

Founded by former boxer and autoworker Berry Gordy Jr., Motown Records became America's largest black-owned entertainment business from the 1960s to the 1980s. Headquartered on Detroit's Grand Boulevard, Motown became known as "Hitsville U.S.A." by generating an impressive string of blockbuster albums. In 1960 Motown introduced Smokey Robinson and the Miracles to America, and their song "Shop Around" quickly rushed to the top of the rhythm 'n' blues charts. Ten months later the Marvelettes' "Please Mr. Postman" became the first Motown song to reach the top of the pop charts. During the next two decades artists like the Supremes, the Four Tops, Marvin Gaye, and Stevie Wonder added to Motown's list of hits, making the company a commercial marvel and an American institution.

The Supremes

Suburbanization

After World War II, returning soldiers came home to a booming economy that included unprecedented new-home construction. Eager to buy homes of their own, millions of families moved out of inner cities and into new "developments" (suburbs) surrounding industrial centers like Detroit. For economic and social reasons, most of these homes were sold to white people, causing suburbs to become excessively white while cities became predominantly black. In spite of this fact, suburbs came to symbolize the American Dream for many people. Their combination of green lawns, single-family homes, and two-car garages reflected the nation's growing prosperity. Suburbs continue to remain popular with many Americans.

MINNESOTA

Nickname: Gopher State | **Capital:** St. Paul | **Statehood:** May 11, 1858 (32nd)
Population: 4,775,508 (21st) | **Area:** 86,943 sq. mi. (12th) | **Highest point:** 2,301 ft. (Eagle Mountain)

Abounding with woodlands, prairies, and lakes, Minnesota enjoys a lush natural environment. Cold in the winter, it is the most northerly of the continental states. Yet Minnesotans maintain a vibrant agricultural economy. The region's rich soil yields excellent crops of corn, soybeans, and wheat. Many livestock farmers raise cattle, hogs, and turkeys for both meat and dairy products. Minerals and lumber supplement the state's economy, but agriculture remains its largest industry.

During the seventeenth century, French explorers traveled across Minnesota's northern border in search of a Northwest Passage through which ships could reach the Pacific Ocean from the Atlantic. Although their search failed, fur traders came to the region and developed a thriving commercial presence. The Louisiana Purchase gave America control of the land that became Minnesota, and the United States made the area an official territory in 1849. White settlers soon conflicted with the Sioux Indians. Driving many Sioux out of the region while confining others in reservations, Americans treated the Indians harshly and dishonestly, signing treaties of their own making and then breaking them. By 1862 the Sioux were fed up. They attacked white settlers in a short but bitter war known as the Sioux Uprising. More than 500 whites and sixty Indians died in this war. Less than a decade later, the Indians had been effectively displaced.

In the twentieth century, Minnesota developed a reputation for radical politics. The state's Farmer-Labor Party pressed for a stronger government role in national life, keeping rural populism alive in Minnesota when it had declined elsewhere. Then, in the 1960s, Minnesota Democratic Senator Eugene McCarthy criticized America's involvement in the Vietnam War. Although his presidential bid stalled, his message gained widespread support and his campaign sustained hope in the American system.

Minnesotans have made strong contributions to American culture. Celebrated authors Sinclair Lewis and F. Scott Fitzgerald were born in Minnesota, and singer Bob Dylan, a Minnesota native, produced a number of songs that evoke the state's populist roots. And from her "little house on the prairie," author Laura Ingalls Wilder introduced the state to millions of American readers.

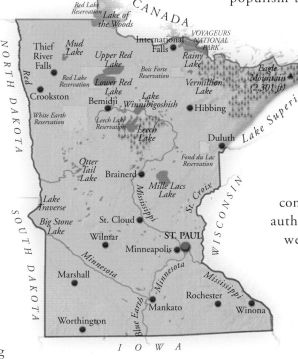

The Anti-Vietnam War Movement

Senator Eugene McCarthy

During the mid-1960s, young people—many of whom rebelliously sported long hair and shaggy beards—began to protest America's war in Vietnam. Young activists organized a number of protests designed to express their disdain for the war and the leaders who waged it. In 1967 Minnesota Senator Eugene McCarthy convinced many protestors to give mainstream politics another chance. Because McCarthy promised to end the war if elected president, thousands of protesters "got clean for Gene." They shaved their beards and cut their hair in order to campaign for him. When McCarthy failed to win the Democratic Party's nomination, many of his followers became disillusioned. Still, McCarthy's anti-war message influenced the thinking of many Americans.

Bob Dylan (b. 1941)

Born in Hibbing, Minnesota, as Robert Allen Zimmerman, Bob Dylan developed a zest for music early in life. During the early 1960s Dylan listened to the music of Hank Williams, Woody Guthrie, Little Richard, and Elvis Presley, and he soon developed his own musical style. After becoming the darling of that era's folk-music lovers, Dylan returned to his rock 'n' roll roots and wrote songs like "Blowin' in the Wind," "Mr. Tamborine Man," and "Like A Rolling Stone" that blended folk, rock, and country melodies. His insightful lyrics and moving rhythms made him the spokesperson for the baby-boom generation. Dylan continues to make music that impresses millions of listeners and influences countless other musicians. He has sold approximately 60 million albums during his career.

Joan Baez (left) and Bob Dylan

MISSISSIPPI

Nickname: Magnolia State | **Capital:** Jackson | **Statehood:** December 10, 1817 (20th)
Population: 2,768,619 (31st) | **Area:** 48,434 sq. mi. (32nd) | **Highest point:** 806 ft. (Woodall Mountain)

Much of Mississippi's soil, especially in the Delta region, is rich and deep and excellent for farming. Its low-lying landscape is laced with many rivers. The Mississippi River itself follows a meandering course along the state's western edge. Dominated by agriculture well into the twentieth century, Mississippi has undergone considerable industrial development. It is home to a number of military bases, and the shipyards in Pascagoula produce naval, merchant marine, and commercial vessels.

During the first decades of the nineteenth century, thousands of settlers migrated to Mississippi in search of land for growing cotton. By 1860 Mississippi was the nation's leading producer of "King Cotton," and black slaves outnumbered their white masters. The second state to secede from the Union, Mississippi was a Civil War battleground. In July 1863 Union forces under General Ulysses S. Grant captured Vicksburg after a forty-seven-day siege. Their victory marked a turning point in the war.

In the years following the Civil War, violence, intimidation, and unfair registration requirements like the poll tax effectively denied Mississippi's blacks the right to vote. As in other southern states, segregation became a way of life. In the early 1960s efforts to challenge segregation and obtain citizenship rights for blacks—led by activists like Fannie Lou Hamer and Robert Moses—were met with violent resistance. In 1961 "freedom riders" (whites and blacks who rode busses together to oppose segregation) were imprisoned in Mississippi for forty-five days. The next year, state officials refused to allow James Meredith, an African-American student, to enroll in classes at the University of Mississippi. Following a night of rioting, Meredith enrolled under the protection of U.S. marshals. More violence occurred in the summer of 1964, when the Ku Klux Klan murdered three young activists who were attempting to register black voters. Those murders—along with that of NAACP leader Medgar Evers a year earlier—helped convince most white Mississippians to accept change peacefully.

Despite the growth of urban areas and the concentration of industry along the Gulf Coast, Mississippi remains a rural state. Its Delta region is famous as the home of American blues music, producing such legendary musicians as Robert Johnson and B.B. King.

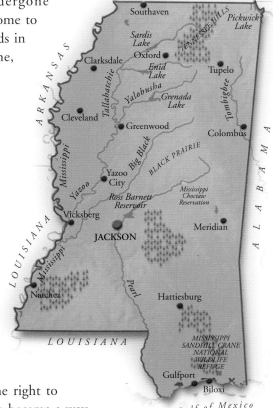

Southern Literature

Eudora Welty

The first half of the twentieth century witnessed the flowering of southern literature. Mississippi natives William Faulkner, Eudora Welty, Richard Wright, and Tennessee Williams were at the center of this creative outburst. In a celebrated series of novels, the Nobel Prize-winning Faulkner created the mythical land of Yoknapatwpha and its brooding, tragic inhabitants. Welty's stories also contain subtle re-creations of southern speech and thought patterns, but she depicted her eccentric characters with sympathetic humor. Wright's books, such as *Native Son* and the autobiographical *Black Boy*, eloquently explored and protested racial prejudice. Set in the South, Williams's plays, like *A Street Car Named Desire*, evoked a remarkable blend of decadence, sensuality, and nostalgia. Taken together, these authors' works fashioned a distinctive southern response to the changing nature of American life.

Mississippi Freedom Democratic Party

Fannie Lou Hamer

During the early 1960s civil rights activists focused on the difficult and dangerous task of local political organizing. Robert Moses, for example, began a voter-registration campaign in rural Mississippi to urge African Americans to vote. In 1964 this effort produced the Mississippi Freedom Summer Project. Part of the project was the formation of the Mississippi Freedom Democratic Party (MFDP), an alternative to Mississippi's white Democratic Party. The MFDP sent delegates—including an outspoken sharecropper named Fannie Lou Hamer—to the 1964 national Democratic Convention. Despite Hamer's moving description of what it was like to be black and poor in Mississippi, the national party rejected the MFDP. This development deepened young black activists' distrust of white liberals and further eroded their faith in the system. It thus contributed to the radicalization of U.S. politics later in the decade.

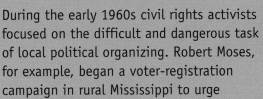

MISSOURI

Nickname: Show Me State | **Capital:** Jefferson City | **Statehood:** August 10th, 1821 (24th)
Population: 5,468,338 (17th) | **Area:** 69,709 sq. mi. (21st) | **Highest Point:** 1,772 ft. (Taum Sauk Mt.)

Near the geographic center of the United States, Missouri represents the gateway to the West for those in the East. The Santa Fe and Oregon trails that brought millions of nineteenth-century pioneers westward ended in the state's largest city, St. Louis. Many of these travelers remained in Missouri to farm corn and cotton. Developers also dammed many of the state's rivers, building artificial lakes and generating hydroelectric power in the process.

During the eighteenth century, French miners, hunters, and traders availed themselves of the region's resources. In the 1760s Pierre Laclede founded the city of St. Louis. Americans poured into the area after the Louisiana Purchase of 1803; even frontiersman Daniel Boone moved his family to Missouri in order to exploit the state's salt deposits. The Missouri Compromise of 1820 focused national public attention on the state. It allowed slavery to flourish in Missouri but outlawed the practice in other areas of the Louisiana Purchase north of the

36°30' latitude. Missouri residents tried to convince Kansans to accept "the peculiar institution" during the 1850s and, when they resisted, border violence exploded. One of the state's favorite sons, author Mark Twain, left Missouri around this time to navigate the Mississippi River and pursue a career in journalism.

World War II brought significant changes to the state. African Americans migrated northward from the Deep South to find industrial jobs, and many of them stayed in Missouri. In 1945 Harry S. Truman, a lifelong Missouri resident, became president and filled his administration with Missouri friends. In 1946 former British Prime Minister Winston Churchill visited the state and delivered a speech in the city of Fulton that announced the beginning of the Cold War.

Most people know Missouri for St. Louis's famous Gateway Arch. Designed by Finnish-born American Eero Saarinen and erected between 1963 and 1965, it is a spectacular architectural achievement that marks the starting point of the American West.

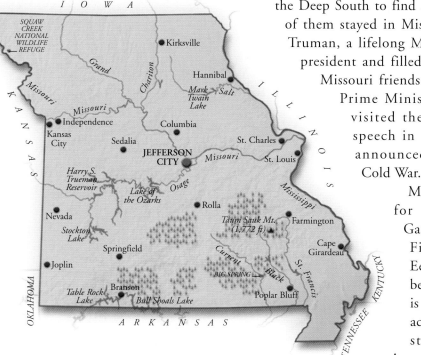

The Dred Scott Case

In 1846 the slave Dred Scott filed suit in a Missouri court in hopes of winning his freedom. He argued that, because his master had taken him into areas where the Missouri Compromise prohibited slavery, he should be freed. In 1857 the Supreme Court decided that Scott, despite having lived in the North, remained a slave. The implications of this decision went far beyond Scott's personal freedom. Northerners were outraged at the possibility that slavery might be permitted in free states (where it had long been banned), and sectional tensions between the North and the South worsened. The Dred Scott case was one of the major factors leading to the Civil War.

Mark Twain (1835–1910)

Born with the name Samuel Clemens, Mark Twain is one of America's most treasured writers. Twain spent his youth in Hannibal, Missouri. There he developed a lasting affection for river life, watching steamboats, keelboats, and lumber rafts flow down the mighty Mississippi. Twain became famous when, in November 1865, he published the story "The Celebrated Jumping Frog of Calaveras County." He soon took a job with a California newspaper and delighted readers with entertaining accounts of his travels abroad. Twain later became a national sensation by publishing *The Adventures of Tom Sawyer* in 1876 and *The Adventures of Huckleberry Finn* in 1884. Late in life, the author slipped into near-poverty. He died in 1910 while writing his autobiography.

MONTANA

Nickname: Treasure State | **Capital:** Helena | **Statehood:** November 8, 1889 (41st)
Population: 882,779 (44th) | **Area:** 147,046 sq. mi. (4th) | **Highest point:** 12,799 ft. (Granite Peak)

The name Montana comes from a Spanish term meaning "mountainous area." And though the western half of the state features some of the most striking mountain ranges in the country, the eastern half is mostly flat with rolling hills. Agricultural ventures account for some of the state's wealth, but natural resources are an even greater asset. Miners and drillers extract coal, oil, and natural gas from the earth, and statewide refineries process these materials. Lumber companies are also profitable, making plywood and paper from western Montana's vast woodlands.

When American explorers Meriwether Lewis and William Clark passed through Montana during the early 1800s, they encountered many Native Americans. Crow, Flathead, and Cheyenne occupied different portions of the state, and these tribes—along with others—competed for supremacy. A small number of trappers and traders followed Lewis and Clark into Montana, but the area's white population significantly jumped when prospectors discovered gold and copper in the area. Immigrants and Indians soon competed for land, and the U.S. Army played a significant role in this conflict.

Native Americans became targets in 1876 as cavalry officers like General George Armstrong Custer pursued them across the Great Plains and into Montana. On June 25, 1876, Custer's 600 men fought 2,000 Sioux warriors along the Little Big Horn River. The Sioux defeated Custer's detachment, and their victory marked the height of Indian power in the nineteenth century.

As Indian power declined, white Montana businessmen attempted to make their fortunes. In the 1890s copper barons like Marcus Daly and William Clark made millions and used their

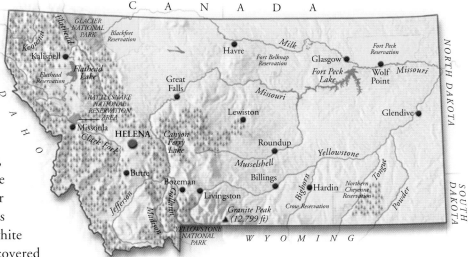

fortunes to gain political clout. Their influence over politicians and labor unions stretched into the twentieth century, weakening only after copper mines slowly petered out.

Montana is not one of America's wealthiest states, but beautiful locations like Glacier and Yellowstone National Parks annually draw great numbers of tourists. By preserving the state's environment, Montana's residents can expect a bright future.

Crazy Horse (c.1842–1877)

Born with the Indian name Ta-sunko-witko, "Crazy Horse" was a famous Oglala Sioux chief who commanded his people at a time when they were extremely powerful. When white settlers and soldiers began to erode Sioux power in the 1870s, Crazy Horse led his people in battle against the U.S. Army. A skilled fighter and strategist, the chief oversaw several successful battles and won acclaim by defeating General George A. Custer at the Battle of Little Big Horn in 1876. American soldiers continued to pursue him, however, and Crazy Horse finally surrendered to General George Crook in May 1877. That same year, U.S. soldiers killed Crazy Horse when he resisted attempts to imprison him in a guardhouse.

The Oglala Sioux tribe surrenders to General George Crook.

Western Writers

During the past thirty years, a distinct circle of Western writers has come of age in Montana. State residents like Norman Maclean, Thomas Maguane, and Rick Bass have produced numerous short stories, novellas, and novels that illuminate the nature of everyday life in the American West. Montana also has provided a lustrous setting for Western writers living outside the state. In 1996 Seattle-based author Ivan Doig wrote *Bucking the Sun*, a novel that depicts life in 1930s Montana and serves as a fine example of how the state's gushing rivers, lush forests, and dank construction sites make excellent backdrops for endearing human dramas. Taken together, such writers have enriched American literature, providing it with a lively and thoughtful new dimension.

NEBRASKA

Nickname: Cornhusker State | **Capital:** Lincoln | **Statehood:** March 1, 1867 (37th)
Population: 1,666,028 (38th) | **Area:** 77,358 sq. mi. (16th) | **Highest Point:** 5,424 ft. (in Johnson Township)

Based on the Indian word for "flat water," Nebraska has rural and urban dimensions. The eastern part of the state holds the city of Omaha, but western Nebraska holds primarily small towns and hamlets. The Platte River and its branches water much of the state, making Nebraska an agricultural powerhouse. Corn and wheat are Nebraska's most lucrative crops, and vast grasslands sustain large herds of cattle.

Nebraska became U.S. territory after President Thomas Jefferson completed the Louisiana Purchase in 1803. In the 1850s Senator Stephen Douglas suggested that Nebraska residents decide whether or not they wanted slavery in the territory (a practice known as "popular sovereignty"), and Congress made his idea law by passing the Kansas-Nebraska Act in 1854.

When the state finally established an organized territorial government just before the Civil War, it became a major highway for human and commercial traffic. Pioneers seeking to make their fortunes farther west passed through Nebraska on the Oregon Trail, and traders determined to exchange goods along the state's Missouri and Platte Rivers established permanent businesses of their own. After the Civil War, railroad construction allowed immigrants to make the most of Nebraska's lush soil and vast grasslands. Thousands of settlers created ranches and farms that produced valuable foodstuffs like meat and corn.

The state's agricultural economy, however, suffered during the 1920s, and the Great Depression of the 1930s made matters even worse. But the onset of World War II in the 1940s increased the demand for agricultural products and caused the central government to encourage the development of industry in the region. The U.S. Government continued to boost Nebraska's economy after the war, making Offutt Air Force Base the center of the nation's newly formed Strategic Air Command. In Nebraska, military officials controlled thousands of bombers and nuclear missiles designed to contain America's Cold War adversary, the Soviet Union.

People drawn to open spaces appreciate Nebraska's landscape. Those who enjoy natural wonders marvel at the state's Chimney Rock, a mountain formation cut into the shape of a chimney by generations of prairie winds.

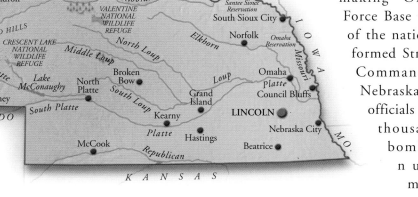

Kansas-Nebraska Act of 1854

Passed by Congress during the presidency of Franklin Pierce, the Kansas-Nebraska Act repealed the Missouri Compromise and, in doing so, erased the old dividing line between free and slave states. It also damaged America's political party system: the Act destroyed the Whig Party, divided the Democrats, and spurred the creation of two new parties, the antislavery Republicans and the anti-immigrant Know-Nothings. In the wake of the Kansas-Nebraska Act, sectional tensions grew stronger than ever, and the Civil War became virtually inevitable.

The Strategic Air Command (SAC)

Established in 1946 to coordinate America's nuclear weapons, SAC controlled thousands of bombers and guided missiles. Its leaders also helped devise the nation's nuclear strategy in ways that reinforced the government's general policy of containment toward the Soviet Union. SAC leaders wanted, first, to prevent the Soviet Union from attacking the United States and its allies with nuclear weapons, and, second, to check the spread of communist theory. The first goal proved easier to achieve than the second. Nevertheless, before shutting its doors in 1992, SAC played an important role in the Cold War.

NEVADA

Nickname: Silver State | **Capital:** Carson City | **Statehood:** October 31st, 1864 (36th)
Population: 1,809,253 (35th) | **Area:** 110,567 sq. mi. (7th) | **Highest point:** 13,140 ft. (Boundary Peak)

Nevada is a Spanish word meaning "snow capped." The Sierra Nevada Mountains that mark the state's California border explain this name, but much of Nevada lies within the Great Basin and the Mojave Desert. Nevada is lightly populated, with residents concentrated in Reno and Las Vegas. Many residents work in the tourist industry, running the casinos that draw millions of tourists each year. Miners also contribute to Nevada's economy, drawing a variety of minerals from the ground. The federal government has a strong presence in the state: it owns thousands of acres of land, operates a nuclear test site, and maintains several military installations within the state's borders.

Humans have lived in Nevada for at least 20,000 years: prehistoric peoples made cave drawings in Nevada's Valley of Fire that are still visible today. Spanish missionaries first visited the area during the eighteenth century, and trappers traced their steps soon after. In 1859 prospectors discovered gold and silver in Nevada's Comstock Lode, encouraging 10,000 miners to pour into

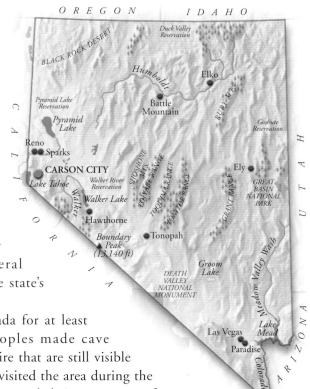

northern Nevada. Expecting the Union to benefit from these minerals, Abraham Lincoln urged Nevadans to apply for statehood. Congress accepted their application in 1864.

Mining and agriculture shaped the state's economy until residents made gambling legal in 1931. Las Vegas and Reno gradually became national attractions, and Las Vegas developed into the state's largest metropolitan area. It has been America's fastest growing city since the early 1990s, drawing waves of new residents into its robust economy. In recent years, gaming executives have changed the city's image by adding family entertainment to increase tourism. Their efforts have cemented the city's reputation as "the Entertainment Capital of the World."

Although people associate Nevada with casinos and "instant weddings," the state is home to many natural and man-made wonders. Red Rock Canyon and Cathedral Gorge State Park showcase striking geological formations, and Lake Tahoe (on the California border) is known as one of the most popular tourist desinations in America. The Hoover Dam, near Las Vegas, exemplifies humanity's ability to harness nature.

Hoover Dam

Built between 1930 and 1936 in Black Canyon on the Arizona-Nevada border, Hoover Dam is the highest concrete arch dam in the United States. It was originally called "Boulder Dam," but was renamed in honor of former President Herbert Hoover during the 1940s. It is 726 feet high and 1,244 feet long, and by generating immense amounts of hydroelectric power, fuels communities across the West. By interrupting the flow of the Colorado River, Hoover Dam created Lake Mead, which is one of the world's largest manmade lakes. An impressive symbol of human industry, Hoover Dam's awesome presence proves that humanity can bring life to the desert.

Las Vegas

Located in southern Nevada, Las Vegas has been one of America's fastest growing cities for the past fifty years. Mormon settlers originally came to the area during the 1850s because its artesian springs allowed people to live in this otherwise arid climate. When state officials made gambling legal in 1931, Las Vegas became especially popular with tourists. People flocked to the city's many casinos and nightclubs in search of good times and easy money. During the 1980s city planners and local businessmen began to develop family forms of entertainment, successfully convincing people to bring their children to the area's resorts. Water shortages threaten Las Vegas's ability to sustain its ever-expanding population. But the city's ability to entertain tourists is unquestioned.

NEW HAMPSHIRE

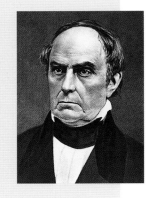

Nickname: Granite State | **Capital:** Concord | **Statehood:** June 21, 1788 (9th)
Population: 1,201,134 (41st) | **Area:** 9,351 sq. mi. (46th) | **Highest point:** 6,288 ft. (Mount Washington)

Within its borders, New Hampshire has the highest mountains in New England, countless lakes and streams, and abundant acres of unspoiled woodlands. Deep glacial gorges formed long ago are common throughout the state. Among the most famous of such valleys is Franconia Notch, which is home to a rock formation known as the "Old Man of the Mountain." Despite its rural appearance, New Hampshire is an industrialized state. For more than a century, its residents have relied on manufacturing as a major source of income and employment.

Several groups of Algonquian-speaking Native Americans inhabited New Hampshire before the first European settlements. Disease, war, and migration quickly reduced their numbers, and by the mid-eighteenth century, most of the surviving Indians had left the region. After the battles of Lexington and Concord in 1775, New Hampshire Minútemen rushed to support the rebels of Massachusetts and the state played a key role in the struggle for independence. In 1788 New Hampshire cast the ninth and decisive vote ratifying the U.S. Constitution. Following the establishment of the nation, the state grew rapidly.

Agriculture—as well as sheep raising—flourished in the state's early years, and manufacturing soon developed along

New Hampshire's fast-flowing rivers. Manchester was once home to the world's largest textile plant. By the beginning of the twentieth century, the state was a leading national producer of shoes, textiles, and wood products. Since World War II, electronics, lumber and pulp industries, and tourism dominate the economy.

A small state, New Hampshire has played a large role in the nation's political history. It produced such prominent nineteenth-century figures as Senator Daniel Webster and President Franklin Pierce. New Hampshire was the site of the 1905 Treaty of Portsmouth peace conference that ended the Russo-Japanese War and earned President Theodore Roosevelt a Nobel Peace Prize. The state also hosted the 1944 Bretton Woods Conference that established the International Monetary Fund. Since 1952 New Hampshire has been home to the nation's first presidential primary. Because it furnishes the initial testing ground for many candidates, New Hampshire attracts tremendous attention every four years.

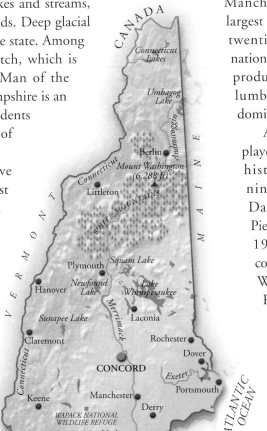

1968 Democratic Primary

In March 1968 Eugene McCarthy, a senator from Minnesota, challenged President Lyndon B. Johnson for the Democratic Party nomination. McCarthy ran as an opponent of the Vietnam War. He argued that America's actions in Southeast Asia were morally wrong. Rallying anti-war activists and students to his candidacy, McCarthy polled 42 percent of the vote to Johnson's 48 percent in New Hampshire's

presidential primary. This near-upset shocked the political establishment and contributed to Johnson's decision, a few weeks later, not to run for reelection. It also gave greater legitimacy to the anti-war movement in the United States.

Eugene McCarthy (center)

Daniel Webster (1782–1852)

An American statesman famed for his oratorical skills, Daniel Webster was born in Salisbury, New Hampshire, and educated at Dartmouth College—also in New Hampshire. Between stints in the House of Representatives, Webster was one of America's leading lawyers, successfully arguing several landmark cases before the U.S. Supreme Court. As a senator from Massachusetts, Webster in 1830 delivered a stirring defense of the Union in response to the Southern states'-rights theory of nullification of national laws. Appointed secretary of state by President William Henry Harrison, he negotiated the Webster-Ashburton Treaty (1842), which settled the boundary between the United States and Canada. Resigning from the cabinet in 1843, Webster returned to the Senate. An opponent of slavery, he devoted himself to efforts to maintain peace between the North and the South.

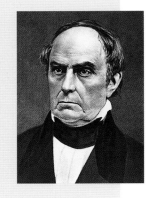

NEW JERSEY

Nickname: Garden State | **Capital:** Trenton | **Statehood:** December 18, 1787 (3rd)
Population: 8,143,412 (9th) | **Area:** 8,722 sq. mi. (47th) | **Highest point:** 1,802 ft. (High Point)

Once famous for its fertile farmland, New Jersey now bustles with commercial life. However, the urban density of its northeast region contrasts sharply with the rugged hills of the northwest, the Pine Barrens in the south, and the rolling countryside in the south-central part of the state. New Jersey's long Atlantic coast contains fine sandy beaches, teeming marshes, and popular summer resorts such as Cape May and Atlantic City.

Named for the island of Jersey in the English Channel, New Jersey was at the center of the Revolutionary War. On December 26, 1776, General George Washington and his hungry, ragged troops crossed the Delaware River from Pennsylvania and defeated a surprised garrison of German mercenaries (the "Hessians") in Trenton. A week later, Washington won another vital battle at Princeton. These victories breathed new life into the colonists' struggle for independence.

Since colonial days, transportation has been at the center of New Jersey's development. In the nineteenth century, the state's network of roads, canals, and rail lines and its proximity to markets attracted industrial titans. By 1875 John D. Rockefeller, the founder of Standard Oil Company,

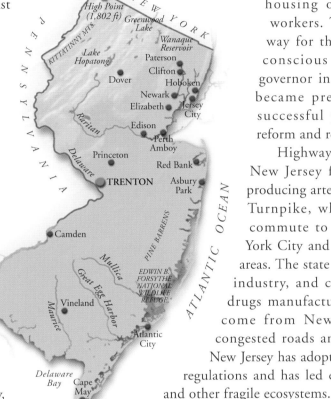

had built refineries in Bayonne; Isaac Merrit Singer had opened a sewing-machine plant in Elizabeth; and Joseph Campbell had established a soup company in Camden. The lives of these wealthy industrialists contrasted sharply with the miserable working conditions and wretched housing of New Jersey's factory workers. This situation paved the way for the election of the socially conscious Woodrow Wilson as governor in 1910. Wilson, who later became president, embarked on a successful progressive program of reform and regulation.

Highway construction boomed in New Jersey following World War II, producing arteries such as the New Jersey Turnpike, which enable residents to commute to jobs in the nearby New York City and Philadelphia metropolitan areas. The state has a large pharmaceutical industry, and close to 20 percent of all drugs manufactured in the United States come from New Jersey. Because of its congested roads and concentrated industry, New Jersey has adopted stringent environmental regulations and has led efforts to reclaim wetlands and other fragile ecosystems.

Thomas Alva Edison (1847–1931)

Born in Ohio, Thomas Edison moved to New York at the age of 21 to work in the financial industry. While in New York, he earned $40,000 by improving the stock market's stock ticker; this success prompted him to become a full-time inventor. Edison set up his laboratory in Menlo Park, New Jersey, where he invented the phonograph in 1877 and the incandescent electric light bulb in 1879. In 1882 he built a steam-based power station that supplied New York City with electricity. Five years later, Edison moved to a larger laboratory in West Orange, New Jersey, where he invented the Kinetoscope, the first machine to produce motion pictures. By synchronizing his phonograph and Kinetoscope in 1913, Edison produced the first talking movies. Altogether, Edison created or perfected hundreds of new devices.

Woodrow Wilson (1856–1924)

In 1902 Thomas Woodrow Wilson, a professor of government, became president of New Jersey's Princeton University. His growing reputation as an effective leader enabled Wilson to win election as governor of New Jersey in 1910. Two years later, he captured the White House. During his first term as president, Wilson passed many progressive laws including those prohibiting child labor and giving workers an eight-hour day. Wilson's second term was dominated by America's entry into World War I. Believing that foreign affairs should be governed by morality and idealism rather than national interest, Wilson helped negotiate the Versailles Treaty that ended the war. Although the Senate ultimately rejected the treaty, Wilson's faith in democracy and humanitarian intervention influenced American foreign policy throughout the twentieth century.

NEW MEXICO

Nickname: Land of Enchantment | **Capital:** Santa Fe | **Statehood:** January 9, 1912 (47th)
Population: 1,739,844 (37th) | **Area:** 121,598 sq. mi. (5th) | **Highest point:** 13,161 ft. (Wheeler Rock)

Touching Arizona, Utah, and Colorado at its northwestern tip, New Mexico forms one-fourth of the "Four Corners," the only point in the United States where four states intersect. Though geographically diverse, New Mexico suffers from a lack of water. Irrigation allows for successful farming, and even more land is used for livestock grazing. Natural resources boost New Mexico's economy: the sale of natural gas and oil produce healthy profits. Miners also drill uranium, making New Mexico a major supplier for the nuclear power industry. Nuclear power research occurs in the state at Los Alamos National Laboratory.

Spanish explorer Francisco Vásquez de Coronado passed through New Mexico in 1540 looking for legendary cities of gold. He encountered Native Americans, as Apaches and Navajos had migrated there during the fifteenth century. After 1821 the area was part of Mexico. The United States, however, won the Mexican-American War and seized the region in 1848. Congress made New Mexico an official territory in 1850, and Union soldiers repelled southern invaders during the Civil War.

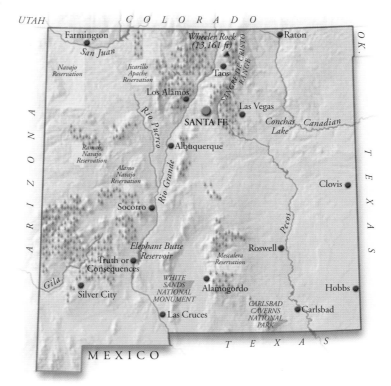

New Mexico became a volatile area after the Civil War. In the 1860s mountain man Kit Carson led troops against Navajos and Apaches, attempting to place them on a reservation. Traditional enemies, the Navajo and Apache did not want to live together on a reservation. Carson defeated the Navajos first and forced them to a distant reservation; the Navajo people labeled this ordeal "the Long Walk." The Apaches, however, fought on before finally surrendering in 1886. New Mexico still possesses a large Native American population: Navajos, Pueblos, Utes, and Apaches continue to live on reservations in the state.

A large number of New Mexicans now live in the city of Albuquerque, but tourists are drawn to smaller towns like Taos and Santa Fe. Visitors also marvel at Carlsbad Caverns, a world-famous natural wonder.

Francisco Vásquez Coronado (1510–1554)

A Spaniard who came to the "New World" in search of riches, Coronado won fame by conquering Indians who resisted Spanish power. He became a successful politician and governed parts of "New Spain" (modern-day Mexico). In 1540 rumors of vast riches to the north caused Coronado to search for the mythical "Seven Golden Cities." Although he never found these places, Coronado did encounter impressive geographic formations in New Mexico and Arizona. In fact, he was the first European to view the Grand Canyon. Coronado returned to his governorship in 1542. He was disappointed with the results of his trip, but Coronado remained a powerful figure until he died two years later.

The Atomic Bomb

The United States began to develop atomic bombs during World War II, hoping that the power of split atoms would help defeat its enemies. The Manhattan Project—an ultra-secret research program—began in 1942 and constituted a massive effort. It led to the explosion of the first atomic bomb on July 16, 1945, at New Mexico's Alamogordo Air Base. Less than one month later, the United States dropped atomic bombs on the Japanese cities of Hiroshima and Nagasaki. The mammoth blasts together killed more than 100,000 people and injured thousands more. The atomic age had begun, and with it came the threat of nuclear war and persistent concern for the safety of humanity.

NEW YORK

Nickname: Empire State | **Capital:** Albany | **Statehood:** July 26, 1788 (11th)
Population: 18,196,601 (3rd) | **Area:** 54,471 sq. mi. (27th) | **Highest point:** 5,344 ft. (Mount Marcy)

From the shores of Long Island and the skyscrapers of Manhattan to the rivers, mountains, valleys, and lakes of the upstate region, New York possesses abundant variety. The most dramatic of the many waterfalls throughout the state is Niagara Falls, one of the most scenic attractions in the country as well as a reliable source of hydroelectric power. The overwhelming presence of New York City has tended to divide the state socially and politically.

Originally settled as a Dutch colony, New York passed into British hands in the 1660s. When Europeans first arrived, two major groups of Native Americans were living in the region: the Mohegan tribe (part of the Algonquian family) and the Iroquois Confederacy (a sophisticated alliance of five tribes— Mohawk, Oneida, Onondaga, Cayuga, and Seneca). With the Iroquois Confederacy's help, the British won the Seven Years' War in 1763, expelling the French from North America after 150 years of struggle.

Since the colonial period, much of New York's growth has been a result of constant waves of immigration, both from other states and from abroad. The Statue of Liberty—a gift from France that was erected in New York Harbor in 1876—was the first vision of America seen by millions of immigrants. Many of these newcomers remained in New York City; others settled upstate. As a result of this influx of people, New York is remarkable for its mixture of ethnicities and cultures. Responding to the demands of this melting pot, New York's leaders— such as Theodore Roosevelt and Franklin D. Roosevelt—have governed in a progressive manner.

New York continues to color much of American economic and cultural life. Manhattan is home to the financial and fashion industries as well as major media outlets— including publishing houses, national magazines and newspapers, and several major broadcast networks. The city's theaters (located on or around Broadway), restaurants, and shops thrive, while its museums— particularly the Metropolitan Museum of Art, the Museum of Modern Art, and the American Museum of Natural History—are models for similar institutions across the country.

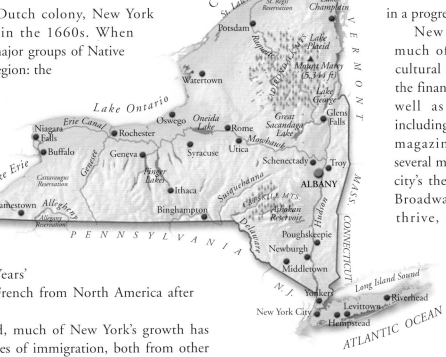

The Seneca Falls Convention

In July 1848 Elizabeth Cady Stanton and Lucretia Mott organized America's first major women's rights convention at Seneca Falls, New York. Over the course of one week, female and male reformers discussed the many injustices imposed on American women. At the end of the convention, Stanton penned a document declaring that, because all people are created equal, women should possess the right to vote. Although women would not win suffrage for another seventy years, the Seneca Falls Convention provided women with a chance to voice their ideas and helped launch a movement that continues to thrive in the United States.

Lucretia Mott

Harlem Renaissance

After World War I, the neighborhood of Harlem in New York City became the center of an African-American creative outburst in art, music, and literature. Poet Claude McKay, a Jamaican immigrant, was the first significant writer of the movement, which celebrated African-American heritage and described the unique experience of being black in the United States. Other prominent writers included Langston Hughes and Zora Neale Hurston. Their work influenced later African-American authors such as Ralph Ellison, Alice Walker, and Toni Morrison. Politically, African-American leaders such as union organizer A. Phillip Randolph took up the Harlem Renaissance's theme of the "New Negro" in their emerging campaign for racial justice.

Poet Langston Hughes

NORTH CAROLINA

Nickname: Tar Heel State | **Capital:** Raleigh | **Statehood:** November 21, 1789 (12th)
Population: 7,650,789 (11th) | **Area:** 53,821 sq. mi. (28th) | **Highest point:** 6,684 ft. (Mount Mitchell)

North Carolina's diverse landscape includes the mountainous west and the gently rolling Piedmont region in the middle of the state. A long chain of dune-covered islands—the Outer Banks—extends along the Atlantic coast. The shallow seas around Cape Hatteras, Cape Lookout, and Cape Fear—the site of hundreds of shipwrecks and pirate activity—have been dubbed the "Graveyard of the Atlantic." North Carolina has a large rural population and is among the nation's leading tobacco and livestock producers. It is also a major source of manufactured goods, such as textiles and furniture.

North Carolina's Roanoke Island was the site of the earliest English attempt to colonize the New World. Known today as the "Lost Colony," it vanished sometime after the original landing in 1587. But settlers soon took root, and from the colonial period to the early nineteenth century, the labor-intensive crops of rice, tobacco, and cotton led to the spread of slavery throughout the state. Unlike South Carolina, whose strident proslavery sentiment led the South into secession, North Carolina left the Union reluctantly. In fact, throughout the Civil War, the state resisted the Confederate government's attempts at central control.

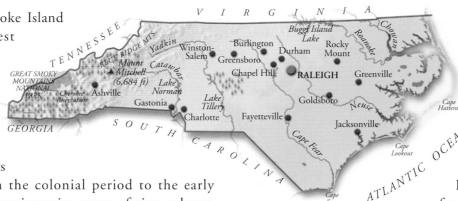

Following the war, North Carolina experienced the economic deprivation and political instability of Reconstruction. Like other Southern states, it enacted laws that effectively restricted blacks to second-class citizenship and kept whites in power well into the twentieth century. The long struggle for racial equality in America entered an important new phase in North Carolina. From its origins at a Greensboro lunch counter in February 1960, the "sit-in" movement spread rapidly throughout the South and spawned the Student Non-Violent Coordinating Committee (SNCC), a leading civil rights organization.

Today, North Carolina is a symbol of the New South, in which modern industry and high-tech farming operations largely have replaced traditional agriculture. Research and development facilities have sprung up—notably in Research Triangle Park, which lies between Raleigh, Durham, and Chapel Hill and was created by three North Carolina universities in 1959. As a result, the number of professional and technology-related jobs has increased dramatically.

The Wright Brothers

In September 1900 at Kill Devil Hill near Kitty Hawk, North Carolina, Orville and Wilbur Wright tested a glider they had invented. Carefully recording their findings, the brothers made almost 1,000 flights over the next two years. On December 7, 1903, Orville took off from the dunes of Kitty Hawk in the first self-powered plane; he stayed aloft for twelve seconds. Five years later, Orville piloted a propeller-driven airplane for sixty-two minutes, while Wilbur set distance and altitude records. Based on the Wright brothers' designs for engines and planes, an American aircraft industry developed following World War I. By 1930 the country had more than forty airlines, which carried nearly 400,000 passengers annually. Along with the automobile, the airplane revolutionized American transportation.

Ella Baker (1903–1986)

Raised in rural North Carolina, Ella Baker developed a sense of social justice at an early age. After graduating from Raleigh's Shaw University, she moved to Harlem, where she joined several activist organizations. In the 1940s Baker worked as a field secretary for the NAACP. Traveling throughout the South, she recruited African Americans to join the organization. In April 1960 Baker—then the executive director of Martin Luther King Jr.'s Southern Christian Leadership Conference (SCLC)—organized and set the agenda for a conference of student activists. Meeting at Baker's alma mater, this conference produced a new civil rights organization: the Student Nonviolent Coordinating Committee (SNCC). Because of her lifelong commitment to civil rights activism, Baker became a role model and cultural hero for young reformers of all races.

NORTH DAKOTA

Nickname: Sioux State | **Capital:** Bismark | **Statehood:** November 2, 1889 (39th)
Population: 633,666 (47th) | **Area:** 70,704 sq. mi. (19th) | **Highest point:** 3,506 ft. (White Butte)

Originally inhabited by a variety of Native-American peoples—including the Chippewa, Cree, Sioux, and Crow—much of North Dakota came into American control when the United States and Great Britain negotiated the Rush-Bagot Agreement in 1817. The state's climate makes it an ideal site for ranching and farming, so residents devote themselves to herding cattle and producing grain. During the 1950s and 1960s the central government pumped money into the state by building military bases and missile silos.

During the nineteenth century a wave of white settlers, many of them European immigrants, came to the state in order to operate farms and ranches. So many arrived that, by 1890, more than 40 percent of the state's population was foreign-born. Confronted with businessmen who set unfair grain prices and charged high fees for using the railroad, these people became politically active in order to protect their profits. Between 1917 and 1921 the Non-Partisan League dominated political life, recommending that the government prevent unfair business practices by owning grain elevators, flour mills, and meat-packing houses. For good reason, many Native American tribes disapproved of such government-run operations. When the federal government began to build dams along Western rivers during the 1930s, it often ignored legal Indian land claims. In North Dakota, for example, the Mandan, Arikara, and Hidasta tribes objected when the government submerged much of their land in dammed water.

Although tourism comprises only a small part of North Dakota's economy, the state possesses great natural beauty. The Great Plains sweep across half the state, rising 400 feet above the Drift Prairie east of the Missouri River, and offering an endlessly striking landscape. The Badlands—a breathtaking array of colorful cliffs and jagged valleys along the Little Missouri River—have drawn admirers for generations.

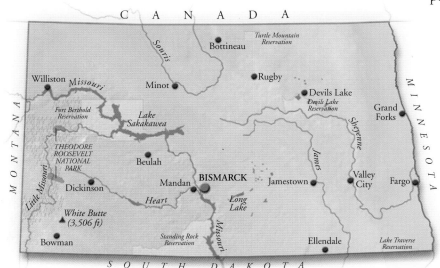

Railroads

The 1850s were a boom time for railroads in America. During this decade, workers laid more than 21,000 miles of track that opened the western United States for population and economic development. The power and speed of the "Iron Horse" thrilled Americans, and railroads became the nation's first billion-dollar industry. Railroad owners, however, often angered residents of western states like North Dakota by charging high prices for use of the rails. A captive audience, farmers and ranchers needed the railroads to deliver their goods to urban markets, and overpriced transportation expenses absorbed much of their profits. As a result, many rural westerners came to regard the railroads as a friend and an enemy.

Populism

During the late nineteenth century, American farmers and workers developed a political philosophy known as "populism" in order to undercut the power of big business. Populist farmers believed the federal government should keep railroad fees low and provide them with cheap loans. Populist workers, on the other hand, wanted the government to guarantee safe working conditions and higher wages. Meeting for the first time in 1890, the Populist Party won substantial influence in many western states. The party, however, could not manage its conflicting interests and disintegrated after six years. Nevertheless, workers and farmers from states like North Dakota still demand that government honor their needs, proving that the populist spirit remains strong.

OHIO

Nickname: Buckeye State | **Capital:** Columbus | **Statehood:** March 1, 1803 (17th)
Population: 11,256,654 (7th) | **Area:** 44,828 sq. mi. (34th) | **Highest point:** 1,549 ft. (Campbell Hill)

Ohio is an Iroquoian word meaning "great water," and the state's strength springs from its natural resources. Farms crisscross Ohio, producing corn, wheat, oats, soybeans, and hay. Farmers also derive profits from beef and poultry. Ohio's mineral, oil, and gas deposits provide satisfying incomes for miners and drillers. Moreover, abundant supplies of clay, shale, and gypsum allow manufacturers to export ceramic goods and industrialists to generate transportation equipment, fabricated metals, and steel.

In the seventeenth century large groups of Native Americans—including the Miami, Delaware, Ottawa, and Shawnee—inhabited the Ohio region. French settlers steadily eroded their power, and the British took control of the region after 1763. Following the American Revolution, Britain ceded to the area to the United States.

Americans rapidly developed a web of railroads, canals, and roads. Citizens crowded into Ohio, making it one of the nation's most populous states. After it entered the Union in 1803, Ohio's large population caused national politicians to heed its needs. In fact, Ohio became the "birthplace of presidents"—William Henry Harrison, Ulysses S. Grant, Rutherford B. Hayes, James A. Garfield, Benjamin Harrison, William McKinley, William Howard Taft, and Warren G. Harding all hailed from the state.

Although Ohioans tend to support conservative politicians, youthful state residents vigorously opposed the Vietnam War during the late 1960s. This dissent turned violent in May 1970. When an anti-war demonstration at Kent State University grew disorderly, National Guardsmen arrived and—in the confusion—killed four students. Racial strife grew in Ohio around the same time. However, when Cleveland's Carl B. Stokes became the first black mayor of a large city in 1968, African Americans saw a needed sign of progress.

Sometimes called "The Heart of It All," Ohio remains a populous state with a strong economy. Urban and rural, Ohio symbolizes American diversity. Its needs are America's needs.

The Gilded Age, 1865–1900

John D. Rockefeller

The U.S. economy boomed between 1865 and 1900, as industries based on oil, steel, and steam produced new wealth. A great deal of financial and political corruption accompanied the booming economy, so many businessmen of this era became known as "Robber Barons." Successful industrialists like John D. Rockefeller, who began his oil-refining business in Ohio, rejected this label, claiming that America's elite deserved its success. Indeed, this new elite proudly displayed its riches, building massive homes and throwing gaudy parties. Some of these parties cost up to $200,000 because hosts provided guests with cigarettes rolled in hundred-dollar bills and food stuffed with jewels. Because everyday problems seemed to be framed in gold during this era, writer Mark Twain labeled it "the Gilded Age."

The Open-Door Policy

In September 1899 the United States attempted to change the way countries practiced foreign affairs. President William McKinley, an Ohio native, had Secretary of State John Hay encourage the world's most powerful nations to relinquish their special claims in China and adopt an "open door" policy that would allow all nations to receive equal treatment from the Chinese government. By early 1900, England, France, Germany, Russia, Italy, and Japan had agreed to respect this "open door," and the U.S. began applying the policy to the rest of the world. Because it leveled the playing field abroad, the open-door policy helped the United States become a world power.

President William McKinley

OKLAHOMA

Nickname: Sooner State | **Capital:** Oklahoma City | **Statehood:** November 16, 1907 (46th)
Population: 3,358,044 (27th) | **Area:** 69,903 sq. mi. (20th) | **Highest point:** 4,973 ft.(Black Mesa)

Oklahoma's terrain varies from the rolling timbered hills of the east to the treeless plains that extend into Texas and New Mexico in the west. The Sandstone Hills, a wide band stretching between the Red River and the Kansas border, are rich in oil and gas deposits. This region is sprinkled with oil-boom towns such as Tulsa. Traditionally a wheat-growing state, oil and gas production has dominated Oklahoma's economy in the twentieth century.

The name Oklahoma is a combination of the Choctaw Indian words for "red" and "people." Throughout the nineteenth century, the region was known as "Indian Territory." In the 1820s the U.S. government decided to move Native American tribes west of the Mississippi River to satisfy white settlers' hunger for land. The resulting "Trail of Tears," as the Indians called their journey, led to Oklahoma. Following the Civil War, many more tribes from Kansas and other western states were relocated to Oklahoma reservations. Lawlessness flourished during this period as criminals—such as Frank and Jesse James—used Oklahoma as a base from which to rob banks, trains, and stagecoaches across the Southwest.

Beginning in the 1880s, railroads and homesteader associations lobbied for white settlement of Indian Territory. In 1889 Congress finally yielded to the pressure and opened two million acres for settlement. At noon on April 22, 1889, more than 50,000 people raced to obtain the land; by evening nearly every lot had been claimed. Earning the nickname "Sooners" for their eagerness, these settlers quickly helped develop the state.

In the mid-1930s, several years of drought turned Oklahoma's fields into dust, which the wind blew into massive dust storms. The Dust Bowl, as it was known, drove thousands of farmers away from the state in search of prosperity elsewhere. Land that was worthless for agriculture, however, often hid large deposits of oil. In the 1970s the federal government began to encourage the revitalization of Native American governments and tribal economies. Thirty-five tribal governments are based in Oklahoma, maintaining a variety of businesses.

The Dust Bowl

During the 1920's, farmers in Oklahoma and other Plains states plowed up grassland to plant wheat. In the mid-1930s the region suffered a severe drought and high winds blew the soil away. Violent dust storms turned the sky black and people had to breathe through their handkerchiefs to keep from choking on the sand and silt. Because of the "Dust Bowl," thousands of farmers and their families emigrated west to California, where they became farmworkers taking low-paying temporary jobs. Made famous by John Steinbeck's 1939 novel *The Grapes of Wrath*, these "Okies" lived in their cars or in camps, usually in miserable conditions. New Deal programs—such as the Soil Conservation Service—helped end the plague of dust storms and ease suffering in the region.

Buffalo Soldiers

More than 180,000 African Americans served in the Union Army during the Civil War. After the war, the future of these troops was in doubt. In 1866, however, Congress passed legislation establishing two "colored" cavalry units—the 9th and 10th—and dispatched them to the western frontier.
Nicknamed "Buffalo Soldiers" by Native Americans, these troops built forts, mapped vast areas of the Southwest, strung hundreds of miles of telegraph line, protected railroad construction crews, subdued hostile Indians, and captured outlaws and rustlers. Although eighteen of the "Buffalo Soldiers" won Congressional Medals of Honor for their service in the West, their contributions to the nation's development were long ignored.

OREGON

Nickname: Beaver State | **Capital:** Salem | **Statehood:** February 14, 1859 (33rd)
Population: 3,316,154 (28th) | **Area:** 98,386 sq. mi. (9th) | **Highest point:** 11,239 ft. (Mount Hood)

Geographically divided, western Oregon possesses rain forests and green valleys while eastern Oregon consists of arid deserts. To the south, lava plains contain small volcanoes and spacious basins. Located near the city of Portland, Mount Hood overlooks the state; at 11,239 feet, it marks Oregon's highest point. Oregon's farmers produce dairy products and cash crops. However, forestry defines the state's economy. Along with products like plywood, wood pulp, and paper, much of America's lumber comes from the state. Industry became prominent in Oregon during World War II, and the technology industry currently fuels the economies of cities like Portland, Eugene, and Salem.

Spanish sailors visited the Oregon coast in the sixteenth century, hoping to find a Northwest Passage that would connect the Pacific and Atlantic oceans. But Britain took a lasting interest in the region during the late 1700s, developing a profitable fur trade. Americans envied this practice, so John Jacob Astor founded the American Fur

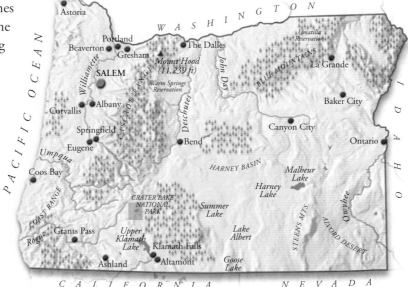

Company and shipped furs from Oregon to his shop in New York City. Settlers followed trappers into the region along the Oregon Trail. Stretching from Independence, Missouri, to Oregon's Columbia River, the Oregon Trail brought thousands of people westward before railroads opened up the state in 1883.

During the early twentieth century, Oregon politicians advanced America's Progressive Movement. Determined to protect workers and bolster democracy, figures like Republican William S. U'Ren forged the Oregon System. This progressive form of politics promoted "initiatives" (a direct vote on issues that people petition to place on voting ballots) and "referenda" (a process in which citizens vote on bills referred to them by their elected representatives). These concepts influenced politicians across the West.

Although businessmen have turned profits in Oregon for generations, the state's lush landscape has caused many environmentalists to live there. For different reasons, tourists fond of hiking, windsurfing, skiing, and fishing make the state their second home.

John Jacob Astor (1763–1848)

A shrewd businessman, John J. Astor opened a New York City fur-goods store in 1786 and quickly built a vast financial empire. After founding the American Fur Company in 1808, he developed a thriving fur trade. Astor's company trapped animals around the Great Lakes and in the Oregon Territory. Astor then sold these furs along the Atlantic Seaboard and in Asia. He became such a powerful figure that one of Oregon's cities, Astoria, bears his name. Astor increased his fortune by speculating in New York City real estate, and used his profits to open a family foundation that still bears his name. To this day, the name Astor conjures visions of wealth.

The Lewis and Clark Expedition (1804–1806)

Even before President Thomas Jefferson doubled America's size by organizing the Louisiana Purchase in 1803, he ordered Captain Meriwether Lewis and Lieutenant William Clark to explore what became the American Midwest and West. Leading a band of roughly forty adventurers, Lewis and Clark

Meriwether Lewis   *William Clark*

traveled through St. Louis, up to North Dakota, and over to the Oregon Coast. While camping in North Dakota, they hired a French-Canadian interpreter, Toussaint Charbonneau, and his Indian wife, Sacajawea. These interpreters helped Lewis and Clark interact with Native American tribes as they moved across the country. The maps and reports that the expedition produced were invaluable. They helped people understand what the frontier actually looked like and who lived there.

PENNSYLVANIA

Nickname: Keystone State | **Capital:** Harrisburg | **Statehood:** December 12, 1787 (2nd)
Population: 11,994, 016 (6th) | **Area:** 46,058 sq. mi. (33rd) | **Highest point:** 3,213 ft. (Mount Davis)

Pennsylvania benefits from rich farmland, abundant natural resources, and a strategic location. Many of its rivers and streams flow through mountainous regions, cutting spectacular gorges and water gaps. The Great Valley—a gentle, rolling lowland that was important in America's early westward movement—extends from the Maryland border in the state's southwest to the Delaware River in the northeast. Small narrow valleys and ragged, broken ridges cover more than half of the state.

Founded by Quaker William Penn as a "Holy Experiment," Pennsylvania's policies of religious tolerance and participatory government encouraged vigorous settlement. By the eve of the American Revolution, Philadelphia was the largest city in North America and the center of the colonial world. The first and second Continental Congresses, as well as the Constitutional Convention, met in Philadelphia. And the Declaration of Independence—which marked the official start of the American Revolution—was signed there.

Farming, lumbering, manufacturing, and the trade of goods made up Pennsylvania's early economy. In the 1820s mining companies began to exploit the state's vast deposits of coal. Used to power the massive steel mills in Bethlehem and Pittsburgh, coal profoundly affected Pennsylvania's economic and cultural development. In 1859 the discovery of oil in the northwestern part of the state changed the face and economy of America. Throughout the second half of the nineteenth century, Pennsylvania's laborers performed long and dangerous work in the coal mines, steel plants, oil refineries, and on railroads. They lived under harsh conditions controlled by their employers. Joining unions such as the Knights of Labor, workers sought higher wages, shorter hours, and safer working conditions. Confrontations between companies and labor unions ensued; the railroad and steel industries witnessed violent strikes in 1877 and 1892, respectively. In 1902 the United Mine Workers went on strike for five months. The strike ended when President Theodore Roosevelt intervened, forcing the mine owners to negotiate and setting a pattern for nonviolent arbitration between labor and management.

Pennsylvania continues to be an important center of industry and manufacturing, while national shrines such as Independence Hall, the Liberty Bell, and Valley Forge National Park are reminders of the state's importance to American history.

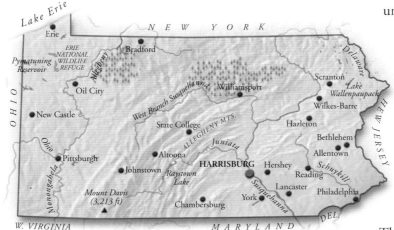

Benjamin Franklin (1706–1790)

A printer by trade, Benjamin Franklin moved to Philadelphia from Boston. By age 23 he was publishing the *Pennsylvania Gazette*. Three years later, he began *Poor Richard's Almanack*. Full of useful information, quips, adages, and practical philosophy, *Poor Richard's* was enormously popular throughout the colonies. After helping to draft the Declaration of Independence, Franklin drew on his considerable diplomatic experience during the Revolution to win a French alliance. At war's end he helped negotiate the peace treaty with Great Britain. Throughout his long and distinguished life, Franklin engaged in many public projects, founding what was probably the first public library in America as well as the University of Pennsylvania. An accomplished scientist, he invented the lightning rod after performing his celebrated electricity experiment with a kite in 1752.

John Wanamaker (1838–1922)

In 1869 John Wanamaker used his experience as a salesman in a men's clothing store to open John Wanamaker and Company in Philadelphia. Wanamaker changed America's retail business; his store featured a wide variety of merchandise, clearly marked prices, and a return policy. A well-known innovator, he used advertising campaigns to attract customers. The success of department stores like Wanamaker's during the late nineteenth century reflected America's increasing urban population, bolstered new mass-production methods, improved transportation systems, and supported the emergence of a prosperous middle class. By the time Wanamaker died, department stores were selling billions of dollars worth of merchandise. Since then, many stores—such as Macy's, J.C. Penney, and Bloomingdale's—have become chains, with branches in large cities and suburban shopping malls throughout the country.

RHODE ISLAND

Nickname: Ocean State | **Capital:** Providence | **Statehood:** May 29th 1790 (13th)
Population: 990,819 (43rd) | **Area:** 1,545 sq. mi. (50th) | **Highest point:** 812 ft. (Jerimoth Hill)

Officially called the "State of Rhode Island and Providence Plantations," Rhode Island is the smallest state in the Union. Its name is misleading since most of the state is part of the North American mainland. Rhode Island, in fact, is the formal name of the largest island of Narragansett Bay, an estuary that extends through the eastern part of the state. Densely populated and highly industrialized, Rhode Island also possesses unspoiled beauty in its Atlantic coastline and in the rolling hills of Block Island, ten miles out to sea.

European settlement of Rhode Island dates from 1636, when Roger Williams founded Providence after he had been banished from Massachusetts because of religious and political conflicts with the Puritans. William Coddington, Anne Hutchison, and other religious dissidents settled additional parts of the colony. This background of dissent and freedom of conscience made Rhode Islanders independent-minded and tolerant of various religious groups and beliefs. In 1772 a group of Rhode Islanders burned a British customs vessel that had run aground, and in 1776 Rhode Island became the first colony to declare its independence from Great Britain. However, the state did not send delegates to the 1787 Constitutional Convention and was the last of the original 13 colonies to ratify the Constitution.

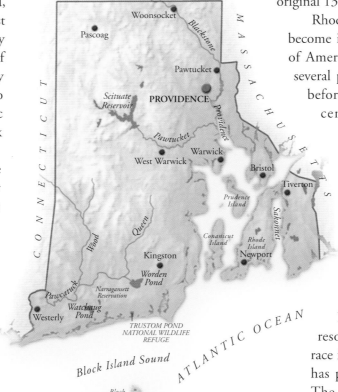

Rhode Island was one of the first states to become industrialized. Providence was the site of America's first successful cotton mill, and several present-day corporations date back to before 1800. Throughout the nineteenth century, Rhode Island's economy—especially the textile industry—continued to expand. Drawn by jobs in the cotton mills and other industries, farmers and thousands of immigrants flocked to cities like Providence. Because it possesses some of the finest harbors on the Atlantic seaboard, Rhode Island has long been popular among sailing enthusiasts. Newport, a fashionable summer resort, hosted the America's Cup yacht race from 1930 to 1983. Rhode Island also has provided a home for the U.S. Navy. The navy maintains several bases in the state and has operated the Naval War College in Newport since 1884.

Anne Hutchinson (1591–1643)

Born in England, Anne Hutchinson immigrated to the Massachusetts Bay Colony in 1634 with her family. She quickly gained great respect among Boston's women as a practiced midwife, healer, and spiritual counselor. Declaring that God had communicated directly with her and that other true believers could also receive God's message without the help of the clergy, Hutchinson gained a substantial following. However, both her religious beliefs and her refusal to accept women's subordinate status offended the colony's strict Puritan leaders. In 1636 she was tried and convicted of sedition, and banished from Massachusetts. A few months later, she and her family followed the route of fellow religious exile Roger Williams to Rhode Island. Inspired by Williams's and Hutchinson's example, groups of dissident Puritans began to settle the state.

Triangular Trade

Before 1808 (the year the United States finally banned the African slave trade) tens of thousands of Africans were forcibly brought to America as slaves. Slave traders had followed the same triangular route for several centuries. They carried rum from distilleries in Rhode Island and other New England states to West Africa and

traded it for slaves. The slaves, shackled in the holds of ships, were taken to West Indian sugar plantations, where they were traded for molasses. The molasses was taken to New England to make rum, completing the triangle.

SOUTH CAROLINA

Nickname: Palmetto State | **Capital:** Columbia | **Statehood:** May 23, 1788 (8th)
Population: 3,885,736 (26th) | **Area:** 32,008 sq. mi. (40th) | **Highest point:** 3,560 ft. (Sassafras Mt.)

The Atlantic Coastal Plain occupies about two-thirds of South Carolina. Included within this flat and swampy "low country" region are the small, sandy Sea Islands. Farther inland, the "upcountry" rises gradually through Piedmont until it reaches the Blue Ridge Mountains in the northwest. Dominated by agriculture well into the twentieth century, South Carolina is also a leading manufacturer of textiles.

Settled in 1670, South Carolina developed a wealthy, aristocratic, and influential colonial society that greatly benefited from slavery. As cotton cultivation spread throughout the state in the early nineteenth century, so did the plantation system. Because black slaves constituted the majority of South Carolina's population, the ever-present possibility of slave revolts—such as Denmark Vessey's aborted uprising in 1822—produced a climate of fear among the white minority.

Increasingly alarmed by Northern attacks on their "peculiar institution" of slavery, South Carolinians took the lead in defending the proslavery position in the decades before the Civil War. The slavery issue, combined with the high tariffs of 1828, precipitated threats of secession in the 1830s. In December 1860 pro-secession radicals (known as "fire-eaters") like Robert Barnwell Rhett led South Carolina out of the Union. The rest of the South soon followed. The Civil War began in April 1861 when Confederate artillery soldiers bombarded Fort Sumter in Charleston harbor. Four years later, after General William T. Sherman's troops had burned their way through the state, the Confederacy surrendered.

In the postwar period, most blacks, along with many whites, became sharecroppers and tenant farmers. In the twentieth century, large numbers of blacks migrated to northern cities looking for work; by 1930 whites made up the majority of the state's residents. In 1948, when the national Democratic Party expressed support of civil rights, South Carolina Governor Strom Thurmond and others formed the short-lived States Rights Democratic Party, or Dixiecrats.

Although some tensions persist, South Carolina has made remarkable progress in the area of racial accord. Today, visitors of all races enjoy the state's many historical sites, Charleston's antebellum charm, and seaside resorts such as Myrtle Beach and Hilton Head Island.

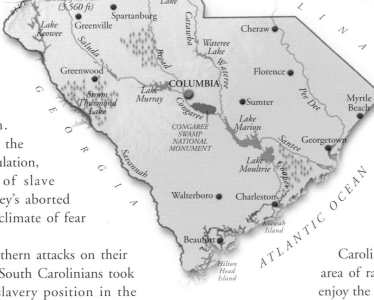

Sharecropping and Tenancy

The Civil War devastated the farms and plantations of South Carolina and the rest of the South. Without slavery, the plantation system proved unfeasible. However, low crop prices made it difficult for blacks and poor whites to own land. Sharecropping and tenancy grew increasingly prevalent as a result. Sharecroppers tilled the land in return for supplies and a share—generally about half—of the crop. Tenant farmers owned their own equipment, and therefore claimed a slightly larger share of the crop. By 1890 the tenancy rate in South Carolina was more than 60 percent. Both systems were inefficient and kept thousands of people destitute and financially trapped well into the twentieth century.

The Changing Nature of Southern Politics

In July 1948 the national Democratic Party committed itself to civil rights for African Americans. In response, defiant southern Democrats rebelled and nominated South Carolina governor J. Strom Thurmond for president on a States' Rights Democratic ticket. Quickly dubbed "Dixiecrats," this pro-segregation party received more than a million votes in the 1948 presidential election and carried South Carolina, Mississippi, Louisiana, and Alabama. The Dixiecrat defection marked the end of nearly 100 years of Democratic dominance of Southern politics. In 1964 Thurmond, by then a senator, formally became a Republican. Four years later, Republican Richard Nixon's "Southern Strategy"—an appeal to white unease over civil rights and related movements—helped him win the presidency. Since then, the Republican Party has thrived in the South.

Strom Thurmond in 1946

SOUTH DAKOTA

Nickname: Mount Rushmore State | **Capital:** Pierre | **Statehood:** November 2, 1889 (40th)
Population: 733,133 (46th) | **Area:** 77,121 sq. mi. (17th) | **Highest point:** 7,242 ft. (Harney Peak)

Named for the Dakota tribe of the Sioux Indians, South Dakota is split into two regions by the upper Missouri River. Its land contains a variety of striking features. The Black Hills—a beautiful set of rolling mounts—rise more than 3,500 feet above sea level and include Harney Peak, a 7,242-foot mountain that is the highest North American point east of the Rocky Mountains. A mixture of Native Americans, whites, and various other groups populate this majestic landscape. Many of these residents raise cattle and sheep for a living, while others run farms, operate mines, and work in tourist industries.

Although French fur traders controlled the region during the eighteenth century, South Dakota fell under American control when President Thomas Jefferson engineered the Louisiana Purchase with France in 1803. Seventy years later, a gold rush caused thousands of settlers to overrun the area. Mining the Black Hills, prospectors ignored legal Indian land-claims and, in 1877, the U.S. Congress forced Indians to surrender their hold on the area. In 1890 tensions between whites and Indians exploded when U.S. cavalry troops massacred 250 Sioux men, women, and children near South Dakota's Wounded Knee Creek. Whites and Indians never fully settled their differences and, in 1973, 200 members of the American Indian Movement (AIM) seized the old battle site. U.S. law enforcement agents surrounded the area and a conflict ensued. One federal marshal was badly hurt and two Indians died before AIM surrendered.

Hard feelings between whites and Native Americans still linger in South Dakota.

Most people associate South Dakota with Mount Rushmore. Initiated in 1927 and completed in 1941, Mount Rushmore is a 6,000-foot stone monument in which the heads of Presidents George Washington, Thomas Jefferson, Theodore Roosevelt, and Abraham Lincoln are carved into the side of a mountain. A symbol of national greatness and a source of public pride, Mount Rushmore annually receives more than 2 million visitors.

Wounded Knee

On December 29, 1890, 400 American soldiers surrounded a group of 200 Sioux Indians near Wounded Knee Creek, South Dakota. Led by Chief Big Foot, these Sioux had abandoned their reservation in order to live according to their own customs. Because they practiced a religion that predicted the extinction of white people, U.S. soldiers considered them dangerous. Thus, when a single warrior failed to surrender his weapon, the American soldiers

killed virtually every Sioux present, including a number of women and children. The tragedy at Wounded Knee not only ended the Indian Wars, it marked the end of traditional Native American life.

American soldiers return from Wounded Knee

James Butler "Wild Bill" Hickok (1837–1876)

Born on May 5, 1837, in Troy Grove, Illinois, Wild Bill Hickok was one of the Old West's most legendary figures. Wild Bill made his reputation as a gifted gunman by working as a sheriff in rough towns like Abilene, Kansas. He became famous when he killed gunfighter Phil Coe in a spirited battle outside Abilene's Alamo saloon. In the end, his reputation caught up with him. On August 2, 1876, Wild Bill was gambling in Deadwood, South Dakota, when a man named Jack McCall approached him from behind and fatally shot him before he could turn around. Deadwood locals buried Hickok in Mount Moriah Cemetery. Captivated by his legend, tourists still visit his grave.

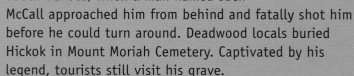

TENNESSEE

Nickname: Volunteer State | **Capital:** Nashville | **Statehood:** June 1, 1796 (16th)
Population: 5,483,535 (16th) | **Area:** 42,146 sq. mi. (36th) | **Highest point:** 6,643 ft. (Clingmans Dome)

Tennessee lies between the Mississippi River in the west and the Blue Ridge Mountains in the east. It is divided into three distinct regions—East Tennessee, Middle Tennessee, and West Tennessee—each with its own culture, economy, and geography. Tennessee is home to several styles of American music, including bluegrass and blues. Rock'n'roll pioneer Elvis Presley hails from Memphis, and Nashville has been the center of country music since 1925, when the "Grand Ole Opry" radio program was first broadcast.

Following the American Revolution, the Cherokee and Chickasaw Indians gradually ceded their lands to white settlers. Led by native-son Andrew Jackson, Tennessee's rough-hewn volunteers won a dramatic victory over the British at the Battle of New Orleans in 1815. Elected president in 1828 and 1832, Jackson strengthened the central government and encouraged westward expansion. Although it was home to some Union sentiment, Tennessee voted for secession in 1861 after the Confederate attack on Fort Sumter. The state paid a price for this decision; only Virginia was the scene of more fighting during the Civil War. Soon after the war, racial violence erupted in Tennessee. The most notorious of the vigilante groups to arise was the Ku Klux Klan, organized in the winter of 1865–1866 by six former Confederate army officers. More than 100 years later, in April 1968, civil rights leader Martin Luther King Jr. was assassinated in Memphis.

Tennessee recovered slowly from the economic ravages of the Civil War. Throughout the late nineteenth and early twentieth centuries, agriculture prices were low and industrial laborers received poor wages and worked under bad conditions. Economic problems worsened during the Great Depression. Tennessee's fortunes finally improved following the federal government's creation in 1933 of the Tennessee Valley Authority (TVA). The nation's largest electric-power generating system, the TVA has improved navigation and controlled flooding on the Tennessee River. It also attracted more industry to the state. Scientists at the Oak Ridge Atomic Energy Research and Development Center, near Knoxville, secretly worked on the Manhattan Project to develop the atomic bomb. Today, Oak Ridge is a leading center for nuclear energy and environmental research.

Reconstruction

Following the Civil War, the nation faced the task of "reconstructing" a ravaged and resentful South. President Andrew Johnson, a Tennessee native, favored a lenient Reconstruction policy. Congressional Republicans, in contrast, wanted to punish the seceding states. In response to the Black Codes—a series of measures adopted by southern states to deny freed slaves citizenship rights—Congress established the Freedman's Bureau, passed the Civil Rights Act of 1866, and adopted the Fourteenth and Fifteenth Amendments to the Constitution. The growing split between Johnson and Congress over Reconstruction policy led to the president's impeachment in 1868. The end of Reconstruction came nine years later when President Rutherford B. Hayes withdrew the last federal troops from the South. During the next several decades, African-American rights crumbled under the pressure of white rule.

President Andrew Johnson

The Scopes Trial

Following World War I, many Americans saw Charles Darwin's theory of evolution as a threat to their religious beliefs. In 1925, under pressure from these "fundamentalists," the Tennessee legislature passed a law prohibiting the teaching of evolution in public

Clarence Darrow (left)

schools. In Dayton, citizens convinced a young high school biology teacher, John T. Scopes, to challenge the law. The resulting "monkey trial" received worldwide publicity and was conducted in a circus-like atmosphere. Clarence Darrow, one of America's leading lawyers, served as defense counsel, and three-time presidential candidate and U.S. Secretary of State William Jennings Bryan appeared for the prosecution. Although Scopes was convicted, the courtroom drama ultimately served to publicize evolution. The Scopes Trial was part of a broader reaction against what many citizens perceived as a frightening new era of diversity and change.

TEXAS

Nickname: Lone Star State | **Capital:** Austin | **Statehood:** December 29, 1845 (28th)
Population: 20,044,141 (2nd) | **Area:** 268,601 sq. mi. (2nd) | **Highest point:** 8,749 ft. (Guadalupe Peak)

Texas's vast and diverse area encompasses forests, rugged mountain ranges, marshes, and flat, seemingly endless stretches of prairie. Underneath the land is a wealth of natural resources. Since statehood, cotton, cattle, and oil have dominated Texas's economic and social development.

In the early 1500s when Spanish explorers first arrived, the region was sparsely settled by various Native American tribes. Over the next 200 years, the Spanish sent more than thirty military and missionary expeditions into Texas, but established only three permanent settlements. In 1821 American Stephen F. Austin received permission from a newly independent Mexico to settle 300 families in Texas. During the next fifteen years, thousands of Americans migrated to the region. These settlers continually clashed with Mexican authorities over several issues, including the Mexican prohibition of slavery. In 1836, after a series of battles, Texas won its independence from Mexico. Although many residents wanted Texas to be a part of the United States, Congress did not approve annexation until 1845. This decision provoked a war with Mexico the next year. Led by Generals Winfield Scott and Zachary Taylor, the United States defeated Mexico and gained control of the land that eventually became the states of California, Nevada, Arizona, Utah, and New Mexico.

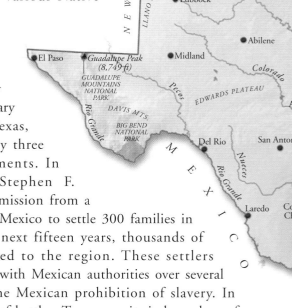

Texas's population and economy boomed after the Civil War. Despite frequent clashes with Comanche, Apache, and Kiowa Indians, settlers streamed into the state. Each year ranchers herded thousands of cattle northward on routes such as the Chisholm Trail, while the cotton crop financed the growth of cities like Dallas and Houston. Large-scale oil production began in 1901; oil and its related industries soon dominated Texas's economy.

Because of its history, many Texans are of Latino descent. And in recent years, legal and illegal Mexican immigration to Texas has swelled the Latino population. Living largely in the cities and towns along the Río Grande River, these residents often speak Spanish in their homes. The mixing of Anglo and Latino traditions has produced a vibrant and influential *frontera* (border) culture.

The Alamo

In 1835 Texas residents tried to break away from Mexico. Mexican leader Antonio Santa Anna raised an army to crush the rebellion. On February 23, 1836, Santa Anna's forces entered San Antonio, and the Texans withdrew to the Alamo, a former Franciscan mission. For thirteen days a small force of 200 defended the Alamo against more than 2,000 Mexican troops. On March 6 the Alamo fell. Nearly all of its defenders—including Davy Crockett and Jim Bowie—died during the brutal battle. Crying "Remember the Alamo," the Texans won the

subsequent battle of San Jacinto and gained their independence. Helped along by films such as John Wayne's *The Alamo*, the battle has achieved mythic status in American history and popular culture.

Lyndon Baines Johnson (1908–1973)

Lyndon B. Johnson worked his way up from a hardscrabble rural Texas background to become president of the United States. As a congressman and senator, LBJ was a masterful politician, often resorting to backroom deals to get legislation passed. As president, he used the momentum provided by his landslide victory to initiate a domestic agenda known as the "Great Society." Designed to achieve social and economic justice for all Americans, this effort was one of the most extensive reform programs in American history. The Great Society proved incompatible with the Vietnam War, however. Disillusioned and frustrated by the war, Johnson declined to seek re-election in 1968. He returned to Texas, where he died in 1973, two years before the last American soldiers left Vietnam.

UTAH

Nickname: Beehive State | **Capital:** Salt Lake City | **Statehood:** January 4, 1896 (45th)
Population: 2,129,836 (34th) | **Area:** 84,904 sq. mi. (13th) | **Highest point:** 13,528 ft. (Kings Peak)

Named for the Ute Indians, Utah possesses canyon-filled plateaus and a basin area distinguished by its desert terrain. Hardscrabble farms pepper the state, and ranchers generate beef and wool. Mining thrives in Utah: the state's Great Salt Lake fuels the processing of potassium, sodium, and magnesium. Manufacturers also contribute to Utah's economy, producing rocket engines, metal products, and transportation equipment, among other commodities.

Native American peoples including the Ute, Shoshoni, and Southern Paiute populated Utah before white settlers arrived. The area became a hub of the fur trade during the early nineteenth century, and, at this time, thousands of pioneers traveled through the state on their way to the West Coast. Members of the Mormon Church, however, made Utah a prominent place when they migrated there after suffering persecution in New York, Illinois, and Missouri.

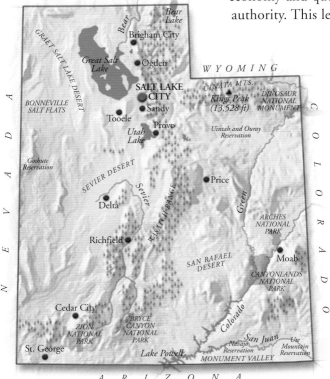

Many citizens disliked Mormon beliefs, arguing that their acceptance of clerical authority threatened America's belief in the separation of church and state. As a result, church leader Brigham Young attempted to make Mormons self-sufficient. He encouraged farmers to sever ties with the national economy and questioned the United States government's authority. This led to the "Mormon War" of 1857. Tired of Young's rebelliousness, President James Buchanan sent 2,500 troops to the territory, causing Young to reach an accord with the central government. Mormons remained powerful players in Utah politics, but thoughts of real independence died.

Contemporary Utah remains a conservative place, and the concept of popular sovereignty still resonates with the public. But Utah has deep connections with the rest of America. Its many ski resorts attract tens of thousands of tourists annually, and the federal government regularly pumps money into the state economy. Although Brigham Young originally hoped to make Utah an independent republic named "Deseret," it is today quintessentially American.

The Great Salt Lake

The largest inland body of salt water in the United States, the Great Salt Lake is Utah's most striking geographic feature. Although it is relatively shallow, the lake covers roughly one thousand miles of surface area, and its waters have a higher salt content than that of the oceans. The lake contributes to Utah's economy by providing a number of valuable minerals and drawing thousands of visitors to area resorts each year. It is one of America's most notable natural wonders.

Brigham Young (1801–1877)

Brigham Young was born in Mendon, New York, but he became one of Utah's most famous residents. When Joseph Smith, the founder of the Mormon Church (the Church of Jesus Christ of Latter-Day Saints), was killed in 1844, Young became the church's leader and remained so for more than thirty years. In 1849 he helped Mormons found the state of Deseret (later called Utah), and served as governor of this territory. His tendency to reject U.S. authority brought him into conflict with President James Buchanan, and he stepped down as governor in 1857. Young's position as church leader, however, made him an influential person for the remainder of his life. A testament to his lasting power, Brigham Young University still bears his name.

VERMONT

Nickname: Green Mountain State | **Capital:** Montpelier | **Statehood:** March 4, 1791 (14th)
Population: 593,740 (49th) | **Area:** 9,615 sq. mi. (45th) | **Highest point:** 4,393 ft. (Mount Mansfield)

Its name derived from the French words for "green mountain," Vermont has thirty-one peaks that rise to more than 3,500 feet, and most Vermonters live in valley hamlets and towns. Vermont's tranquil rural landscape and recreational facilities make the state a popular year-round vacation area. In addition, Vermont dairy farmers, manufacturers, and craft workers supply regional and national markets with specialty foods and products.

A frontier region, Vermont was often a battleground as France and Britain fought for control of North America. In the decade before the American Revolution, residents of New York and New Hampshire also clashed over control of the sparsely populated area. From 1777 to 1791 Vermont was an independent republic. It then became the first state admitted to the Union after the original thirteen. Following statehood, Vermont's population increased rapidly. By the early nineteenth century, however, Vermonters were departing in large numbers for the

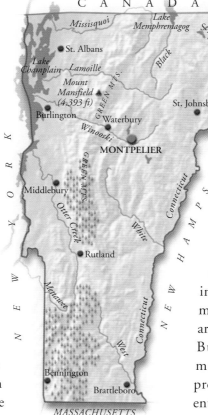

expanding cities and the more fertile lands to the south and west. The opening of the Erie Canal in 1825 and later improvements in transportation hastened this emigration. Vermont's population did not rise again until the development of the recreation and tourism industry following World War II. The first ski trails were built in the 1930s, and today residents and visitors alike enjoy skiing at resorts such as Killington and Stowe. Other popular recreational activities include hiking through Vermont's scenic woodlands and fishing in the state's numerous ponds, lakes, and streams. To safeguard its natural resources, Vermont has passed strong environmental protection laws.

Vermont offers a vigorous cultural life despite its rural and small-town character. Painters find inspiration in the landscape, and sculptors adapt old materials from barns and antique shops into works of art. Such famous literary figures as Sinclair Lewis, Pearl Buck, Robert Frost, and Robert Penn Warren maintained homes in the state. Vermont has also produced prominent Americans such as inventor and entrepreneur John Deere, Mormon leader Joseph Smith, and Presidents Chester Arthur and Calvin Coolidge.

Ethan Allen and the Green Mountain Boys

Ethan Allen (center)

By 1775, although debate continued over whether the American colonies should declare themselves independent of Great Britain, fighting had begun. In addition to the battles of Lexington and Concord, Ethan Allen of Vermont led a volunteer militia—known as the Green Mountain Boys—in a surprise attack against Fort Ticonderoga on New York's Lake Champlain. Originally organized by Allen before the Revolution to oppose New York's claims to Vermont, the Green Mountain Boys, with the help of Benedict Arnold, captured the fort on May 10, 1775. In 1777 the Green Mountain Boys helped the colonials win another decisive victory at the Battle of Bennington.

Hippie Capitalism

The spirit of social responsibility that permeated the 1960s and early 1970s had a profound impact on the way Americans did business in later years. Looking to reform capitalism, activists attacked corporations' products, pollution, and discriminatory practices. Many protestors simply boycotted

Jerry Greenfield (left) and Ben Cohen

businesses they considered unenlightened and established their own enterprises. These entrepreneurs—such as Vermont ice cream manufacturers Ben & Jerry's—demonstrated that the community could profit along with the company. Over the past thirty years, these businesses have increased employment opportunities for minorities and women, invested in local improvement projects, and demonstrated a concern for the environment. Following the lead of these "hippie capitalists," many of today's corporations work to convince the public that they are good citizens.

VIRGINIA

Nickname: Old Dominion | **Capital:** Richmond | **Statehood:** June 25th, 1788 (10th)
Population: 6,872,912 (12th) | **Area:** 42,777 sq. mi. (35th) | **Highest point:** 5,729 ft. (Mount Rogers)

Forests cover nearly two-thirds of Virginia's land, which descends from the mountains of the west to the beaches, tidal marshes, and swamps of the Tidewater region in the east. The northern part of the state reflects the cosmopolitan character of Washington, D.C. Other areas, especially the Shenandoah Valley, retain a more rural flavor. Within its borders lie beautiful national parks and many important historical monuments. These include colonial restorations such as Williamsburg, and many Revolutionary and Civil War battlefields.

Named for Elizabeth I, the Virgin Queen, Virginia has a rich historical heritage. Its Jamestown colony, founded in 1607, was the first permanent English settlement in North America. Jamestown got off to a rocky start but survived because of tobacco cultivation, which the colonists learned from Native Americans. Harvested largely by black slaves, tobacco quickly spread throughout the state and Virginia prospered during the colonial period. Virginians such as George Washington, Thomas Jefferson, James Madison, and James Monroe—four of the first five presidents—provided crucial leadership during America's formative years.

Throughout the first half of the nineteenth century, nearly one-half of Virginia's population was comprised of slaves. Several slave insurrections in the state inflamed and frightened whites throughout the South. Nat Turner's 1831 revolt caused southern legislatures to impose stricter control over slaves and encouraged the abolitionist movement in the North. Seceding with the rest of the South in 1861, Virginia gave great support—including the leadership of Robert E. Lee and other generals—to the Confederate cause. Because Richmond served as the capital of the Confederacy, Virginia was the war's chief battleground.

Well into the twentieth century, racial attitudes in Virginia proved resistant to change. Although the state avoided the violent clashes that characterized the civil rights movement in other parts of the South, the white leaders of Prince Edward County decided to close its schools in 1959 rather than integrate them. By 1989, however, L. Douglas Wilder, a black Democrat, was able to win election as governor. His victory over a white Republican made him the first elected black governor in U.S. history.

Virginia Dynasty

Four of the nation's first five presidents were from Virginia: George Washington, Thomas Jefferson, James Madison, and James Monroe. These men helped create and guide the nation in its crucial early years. Washington, the leader of the Continental Army and America's first president, set the precedents that shaped the position of president. Jefferson's and Madison's words and actions determined the public's understanding of freedom, rights, and responsibilities. The last of the revolutionary generation to become president, Monroe oversaw tremendous domestic expansion and warned Europe against further colonization in the Western Hemisphere. Taken together, the success of these Virginians highlights the political power of the South during the early national period, a fact that later troubled opponents of slavery.

Thomas Jefferson

Washington, D.C.

In November 1800, as a result of political compromise, the nation's capital moved from Philadelphia to the District of Columbia on the banks of the Potomac River. President George Washington chose the specific location along the Virginia-Maryland border, and Congress named the new city after

U.S. Capitol Building

him. For the most part, Washington remained a small town until the mid-twentieth century. Following World War II, both the federal government and the city expanded rapidly. Today, Washington is the core of a major metropolitan area, and the center of national and international affairs. Its most distinctive feature is the Mall, a central open space surrounded by public buildings, museums, and monuments. Because it is the seat of government, the city has been the site of public demonstrations, such as the March on Washington by civil rights advocates in August 1963.

WASHINGTON

Nickname: Evergreen State | **Capital:** Olympia | **Statehood:** November 11, 1889 (42nd)
Population: 5,756,361 (15th) | **Area:** 71,302 sq. mi. (18th) | **Highest point:** 14,410 ft. (Mount Rainier)

Divided into eastern and western regions by the Cascade Mountains, Washington possesses two distinct climates. Rain drenches the western third of the state, which is made up of temperate rain forests. But the eastern two-thirds of the state is hotter and drier: grasslands and hills distinguish this region. Washington's economy reflects this climatic division. Western Washington traditionally has depended on forestry, fishing, and shipping, although in recent years information and technology industries have taken root near Seattle, the state's largest city. Eastern Washington is more agricultural, with crops, livestock, and dairy products providing the region's wealth.

Native American peoples including the Chinook, Cayuse, and Makah had long enjoyed Washington's abundant hunting and fishing opportunities when white explorers moved into the region. During the eighteenth and nineteenth centuries, Great Britain and the United States fiercely competed for control of this territory. However, when Manifest Destiny captured the American imagination during the 1840s, the U.S. government diligently worked to take control of the area. American settlers responded by pouring into the region, pushing Britain and the United States to the brink of war. After a series of heated negotiations, British diplomats in 1846 surrendered the land that became the states of Washington and Oregon.

Radical politics soon developed in Washington. In 1896 utopian socialists opened a 280-acre communal settlement named "Equality." Like similar groups across the West, this one hoped to make the region a refuge from capitalist development. They failed, but radical politics remained influential in Washington. In 1919 the Central Labor Council led a general strike in Seattle that supported local shipyard workers. It paralyzed the city for four days but collapsed without achieving lasting reform.

Washington dominated the national news in 1980 when Mount St. Helens, a volcano near the Oregon border, erupted and spit massive clouds of ash into the air. But Mount Rainier, the fifth highest peak in the continental United States, better symbolizes the state's scenic beauty.

Microsoft

Bill Gates

Based in Redmond, Washington, the Microsoft Corporation has become one of the most powerful companies in the world. When William H. Gates and Paul G. Allen created an operating system capable of powering the nation's growing number of personal computers, businesses across the world purchased it and made Microsoft—named after microcomputers and the software that ran them—an exceedingly profitable venture. Microsoft steadily improved its products, manufacturing the Windows operating system and the Explorer Web browser during the 1990s. In fact, Microsoft has become so dominant that a federal judge recently deemed it a monopoly and ordered the company be broken into two separate enterprises. Microsoft disputed the decision and remains a powerful presence in the Information Age.

Manifest Destiny

1848 Democratic presidential candidate Lewis Cass

In July 1845 John L. O'Sullivan published an article in *The United States Magazine and Democratic Review* that claimed it was America's "manifest destiny" to claim the North American continent for itself. This popular term served as a rallying cry for citizens interested in gaining new land for the United States by annexing Texas, waging war on Mexico, claiming Native American territories, and challenging Great Britain's control over areas that became the states of Washington and Oregon. Those who believed in the idea of "manifest destiny" argued that America's political and religious institutions were uniquely virtuous. Because they believed that the spread of American political culture promised to uplift all of humanity, they turned a blind eye to the suffering that this expansion inflicted upon other peoples.

WEST VIRGINIA

Nickname: Mountain State | **Capital:** Charleston | **Statehood:** June 20, 1863 (35th)
Population: 1,806,928 (36th) | **Area:** 24,231 sq. mi. (41st) | **Highest point:** 4,861 ft. (Spruce Knob)

Lying in the heart of the Appalachian Mountains, West Virginia is the highest U.S. state east of the Mississippi River. The state is tied economically and culturally to the mountain spines that span its length and breadth. For decades, its rich coal beds and fields of natural gas and oil made West Virginia a leading producer of American energy. The gnarled terrain, however, serves to cut off much of West Virginia from surrounding areas. Locked in narrow valleys, some residents retain the customs and speech patters of a much earlier time.

Part of Virginia until the Civil War, West Virginia was only sparsely settled during the colonial period; its mountain ranges proved an effective barrier to expansion. The development of the steamboat and the construction of the National Road to Wheeling in 1818 helped open the area to settlement. By 1860 West Virginia was a land of small farms and growing commerce. Partly because the region was unsuited for slavery, its residents had long resented the wealthy plantation elite east of the mountains. Culturally and economically, West Virginians were closer to Pennsylvanians and Ohioans than to Southerners. When Virginia followed other Southern states in seceding from the Union in 1861, the western counties chose instead to form a new state. Congress approved the admission of West Virginia to the Union on June 20, 1863.

The increased demand for its natural resources transformed West Virginia in the late nineteenth century. Railroads expanded into nearly every part of the state, and residents tapped previously untouched timber acres and coal fields. New scientific methods of drilling sparked an oil and natural gas boom. Large numbers of immigrants from southern and eastern Europe arrived to work the state's extractive industries. West Virginia's industrial boom was accompanied by labor unrest, especially in the coal mines, where wages remained low and working conditions were poor and dangerous. The worst disaster, an explosion at Monongah in 1907, killed 361 people. Following World War II, the increasing mechanization of mining resulted in vast unemployment and deprivation throughout the state. In recent years, progressive government efforts have improved social and economic conditions. The state has also made efforts to diversify its industrial base and preserve its resources.

John Brown (1800–1859)

During his years of scraping out a living as a tanner in Pennsylvania and Ohio, John Brown—a white man—became an antislavery activist. Fired by religious zeal, Brown and his family killed five proslavery men in Kansas in 1856. Brown then spent three years plotting the capture of the federal armory at Harpers Ferry. Although he seized the arsenal on October 16, 1859, federal troops led by Robert E. Lee soon overcame him. Nearly half of his twenty-two men were killed, including two sons. Brown was captured, tried, and hanged for treason. Northerners responded to his death with admiration and sympathy. Outraged southerners concluded that abolitionists would stop at nothing to free the slaves.

McCarthyism

On February 9, 1950, in Wheeling, West Virginia, U.S. Senator Joseph McCarthy declared that more than 200 members of the Communist party secretly held positions in the U.S. government. Although McCarthy could not prove that a communist conspiracy to overthrow the government actually existed, he used live

Senator Joseph McCarthy (standing)

television hearings between April and June 1954 to ruin the reputations of several innocent people. As time passed, McCarthy's accusations became increasingly wild, and his fellow senators condemned him. Still, McCarthy tapped into the Cold War fears of millions of Americans and created an atmosphere of paranoia inside the United States known as "McCarthyism."

WISCONSIN

Nickname: Badger State | **Capital:** Madison | **Statehood:** May 29, 1848 (30th)
Population: 5,250,446 (18th) | **Area:** 65,499 sq. mi. (23rd) | **Highest point:** 1,951 ft. (Timms Hill)

Known for its cheese, Wisconsin has a diverse economy. Its southeastern sector supports a number of industrial plants that produce metal goods and process paper products. Southern Wisconsin, however, enjoys the mild climate and rich soil needed for agricultural success. Farmers in this region produce dairy products like milk, butter, and, of course, cheese.

Tourists also flock to Wisconsin, taking advantage of the state's many wooded areas and scenic lakes. State parks and public forests make ideal sites for vacationers seeking the pleasures of the great outdoors.

Wisconsin's deer, rabbits, beavers, and bears had sustained Indians for generations, and they attracted French trappers during the eighteenth century. When Americans gained control of the

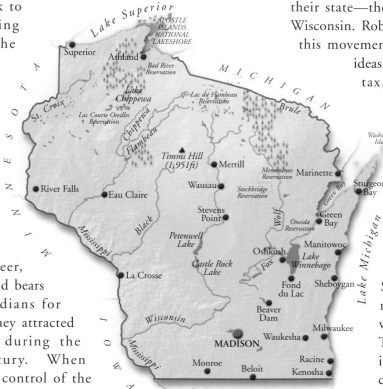

area in 1783, they focused on exploiting Wisconsin's forests and mineral deposits. The lumber industry leveled much of the state's northern woodlands in the late nineteenth century, and miners shipped tons of ore out of the state before depleting reserves in the 1960s.

In the first two decades of the twentieth century—as workers and farmers came to resent the growing power of big business in their state—the Progressive Movement gained momentum in Wisconsin. Robert M. La Follette Sr. was one of the leaders of this movement. As governor, La Follette turned progressive ideas into political policy. He imposed a state income tax, reformed business practices, and signed a worker's compensation act. Elected to the U.S. Senate in 1906, "Fighting Bob" championed progressive ideas from this location. The senator designed legislation that improved working conditions for sailors and increased passenger safety on American ships. He also consistently opposed the pro-business policies of President William Howard Taft.

During the 1950s another Wisconsin Senator, Joseph McCarthy, sullied the state's reputation by loudly accusing people—many of whom were innocent—of being communist spies. Today, Wisconsin retains its reputation for independent thinking and progressive politics in contemporary America.

Student Activism

During the 1960s American students tried to effect political reforms based on an appreciation of equality and justice. Students from major universities like the University of Wisconsin, Madison, for example, worked in the civil rights movement, and many of the women involved in this struggle eventually argued that females deserved real equality as well. Furthermore, university students who opposed the Vietnam War joined organizations like Students for a Democratic Society and demanded that the national government stop the war. Although students did not achieve all of their goals, they did change America. The country is more hospitable to minority groups and women largely because of their efforts.

Progressivism

An authentic American reform movement, Progressivism suggested that government should play an important role in improving society. Some of the issues that concerned Progressives were child labor, unsanitary industrial conditions, the conservation of natural resources, and the abuse of power by big business. "Muckrakers"—journalists like Ida Tarbell and Lincoln Steffens—wrote articles that exposed corruption in both politics and business, and their efforts helped rally support for Progressive causes. Career politicians also advanced Progressivism—President Theodore Roosevelt made a great show of breaking up monopolies that threatened to crush small businesses, and Wisconsin's Robert LaFollette focused on reducing the power of railroad barons.

Robert LaFollette and grandchild

WYOMING

Nickname: Equality State | **Capital:** Cheyenne | **Statehood:** July 10, 1890 (44th)
Population: 479,602 (50th) | **Area:** 479,602 sq. mi. (10th) | **Highest Point:** 13,804 ft. (Gannett Peak)

The name Wyoming derives from an Indian word meaning "great plains." The cities of Cheyenne and Casper hold much of the state's sparse population, while other residents live in small towns and in vast rural areas. Agriculture represents a major part of Wyoming's economy. Ranchers raise cattle and sheep, and farmers grow grains, beans, and potatoes. Mining has become increasingly important in Wyoming. Oil, gas, and coal provide valuable sources of fossil-fuel energy, and the state's uranium deposits contribute to America's nuclear power industry. The U.S. government has a lot to say about how land is used in Wyoming: it owns nearly 50 percent of the state.

Before white people came to Wyoming, a host of Native American peoples lived there, hunting massive herds of buffalo for sustenance. The Shoshoni were the largest tribe, but Arapaho, Crow, Cheyenne, and Sioux were also present. When white settlers came to Wyoming, they came in droves, but few of them remained. Between the 1840s and 1860s, more than 400,000 people passed through Wyoming on their way to other western states.

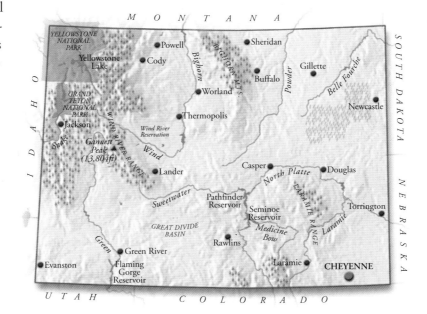

When the Union Pacific Railroad reached Cheyenne in 1867, people began to settle there, and residents soon acquired various-sized cattle ranches. Unfortunately, violence broke out when large-ranch owners and small-ranch owners could not resolve their differences. Large ranchers formed the Wyoming Stockgrowers Association and used the organization to crush their competitors. In 1891 Association members organized a "lynching bee," hanging innocent small ranchers whom they falsely accused of being rustlers. State politics calmed as time passed and, in 1924, Wyoming voters made Nellie Tayloe Ross the nation's first female governor.

Wyoming remains sparsely populated, but skiing thrives in the town of Jackson Hole, and Yellowstone and Grand Teton National Parks inspire millions of visitors annually. Nicknamed the "Cowboy State" for its ranching roots, Wyoming offers a variety of exciting activities for those who appreciate open spaces.

Philip H. Sheridan (1831–1888)

A graduate of the United States Military Academy at West Point, Sheridan became a famous general during the Civil War. When the war began, he commanded Union forces in Tennessee and Ohio. Because he performed impressively there, General Ulysses S. Grant moved Sheridan eastward in 1864 and bid him to pressure General Robert E. Lee's failing Confederate forces. In 1865 Sheridan helped pin Lee near Appomattox, Virginia, contributing to Lee's decision to surrender. Sheridan then waged a series of Indian wars in the American West and earned a reputation for brutality. He became the army's commanding general in 1883 following the retirement of his predecessor, General William T. Sherman. Sheridan's campaigns took him through Wyoming, and one of the state's cities now bears his name.

Buffalo

When white settlers moved west, they encountered massive herds of buffalo. These large animals had crossed the Great Plains and Black Hills for generations, providing numerous Indian tribes with a precious source of food and clothing. But, because their meat and hides proved extremely profitable, white settlers and traders hunted them to the point of near-extinction, often leaving their skinned carcasses to rot on the plains. In doing so, they deprived the Indians of a valuable source of food and contributed to their collective downfall. Buffalo still roam parts of the United States, but they have never returned to their original numbers.

Photography and Picture Credits

Cover photos:
Pearl Harbor: Franklin D. Roosevelt Library
Wright Brothers' flyer: Library of Congress
Statue of Liberty: Corbis

Maps: cover and interior: © 2001 Digital Wisdom
Publishing Ltd., cartography by Nicholas Rowland

Alabama, page 6
Selma skyline: Selma and Dallas County, Alabama
Economic Development Authority
Helen Keller: Library of Congress

Alaska, page 7
Rachel Carson: AP/Wide World Photos
William H. Seward: National Archives and Records
Administration

Arizona, page 8
Barry Goldwater: AP/Wide World Photos
Chief Geronimo: Library of Congress

Arkansas, page 9
Little Rock skyline: Little Rock Convention and
Visitors Bureau
William Fulbright: LBJ Library, photo by Yoichi Okamoto
Hillary Rodham Clinton: courtesy of the office of Senator
Hillary Rodham Clinton

California, page 10
San Francisco earthquake ruins: Library of Congress
Hollywood: AP/Wide World Photos

Colorado, page 11
John Wesley Powell: National Archives and Records
Administration

Connecticut, page 12
Harriet Beecher Stowe: National Archives and Records
Administration

Delaware, page 13
Fenwick Island Lighthouse: Bethany-Fenwick Area
Chamber of Commerce
Caesar Rodney quarter: courtesy of the U.S. Mint

Florida, page 14
Apollo 11: NASA

Georgia, page 15
Coca-Cola headquarters: AP/Wide World Photos
Ted Turner: AP/Wide World Photos

Hawaii, page 16
Pearl Harbor: Franklin D. Roosevelt Library

Idaho, page 17
Ernest Hemingway: AP/Wide World Photos
William E. Borah: AP/Wide World Photos

Illinois, page 18
Democratic National Convention demonstrations:
AP/Wide World Photos
Children at Hull House: Jane Addams collection,
Swarthmore College Peace Collection

Indiana, page 19
Albert Beveridge: Library of Congress
Indiana University basketball: AP/Wide World Photos

Iowa, page 20
Amana Colonies woolen mill: Amana Colonies
Convention and Visitor's Bureau
Herbert Hoover: National Archives and Records
Administration

Kansas, page 21
Kansas State Capitol: Greater Topeka Chamber
of Commerce
Dwight David Eisenhower: Library of Congress

Kentucky, page 22
Abraham Lincoln: Library of Congress
Political cartoon depicting the capture of Jefferson Davis:
Library of Congress

Louisiana, page 23
Mahalia Jackson at the New Orleans Jazz Festival:
AP/Wide World Photos

Maine, page 24
Joshua Chamberlain: Library of Congress

Maryland, page 25
H.L. Mencken: Brown Brothers
Frederick Douglass: National Archives and Records
Administration

Massachusetts, page 26
Margaret Fuller: Brown Brothers
W.E.B. Du Bois: Library of Congress

Michigan, page 27
Supremes: AP/Wide World Photos

Minnesota, page 28
Eugene McCarthy: AP/Wide World Photos
Bob Dylan: National Archives and Records Administration

Mississippi, page 29
Eudora Welty: Library of Congress
Fannie Lou Hamer: AP/Wide World Photos

Missouri, page 30
Mark Twain: Running Press Archive

Montana, page 31
Crazy Horse and tribe leaving Camp Sheridan to
surrender to General Crook: Library of Congress

Nebraska, page 32
Strategic Air Command: AP/Wide World Photos

Nevada, page 33
Hoover Dam: National Archives and Records
Administration

New Hampshire, page 34
1968 Democratic Primary candidate Eugene McCarthy:
AP/Wide World Photos
Daniel Webster: National Archives and Records
Administration

New Jersey, page 35
Thomas Edison: Library of Congress
Woodrow Wilson: Library of Congress

New Mexico, page 36
"Trinity" explosion at Los Alamos, Alamogordo, NM:
National Archives and Records Administration

New York, page 37
Lucretia Mott: Library of Congress
Langston Hughes: AP/Wide World Photos

North Carolina, page 38
Wright Brothers' flyer: Library of Congress

North Dakota, page 39
Badlands: North Dakota Tourism Department
Railroad: State Historical Society of North Dakota,
photo 0032-RI-15-04

Ohio, page 40
John D. Rockefeller: Library of Congress
William McKinley: Library of Congress

Oklahoma, page 41
Buffalo Soldiers: Montana Historical Society, Helena

Oregon, page 42
Meriwether Lewis: Independence National Historical Park
William Clark: Independence National Historical Park

Pennsylvania, page 43
Benjamin Franklin: National Archives and Records
Administration
John Wanamaker: Brown Brothers

Rhode Island, page 44
Anne Hutchinson: Brown Brothers
Africans on deck of slave ship, "Wildfire": Library of
Congress

South Carolina, page 45
J. Strom Thurmond: AP/Wide World Photos

South Dakota, page 46
Return of Casey's scouts from the fight at Wounded Knee:
National Archives and Records Administration
Wild Bill Hickok: Brown Brothers

Tennessee, page 47
Andrew Johnson: Library of Congress
Clarence Darrow at Scopes Trial: Library of Congress

Texas, page 48
Battle of the Alamo: Library of Congress
Lyndon B. Johnson: LBJ Library, photo by Yoichi
Okamoto

Utah, page 49
Great Salt Lake: National Archives and Records
Administration
Brigham Young: used by permission, Utah State
Historical Society, all rights reserved, photo no. 14357

Vermont, page 50
West Dover, VT: photo © Jeff Dickson, Southern
Vermont Adventures
Ethan Allen at Ticonderoga: Library of Congress
Ben & Jerry: AP/Wide World Photos

Virginia, page 51
Thomas Jefferson: Library of Congress

Washington, page 52
Bill Gates: © 2000 Microsoft Corporation photo
Caricature of Democratic presidential candidate,
Lewis Cass, suggesting that his expansionist leanings
would lead the US into war: Library of Congress

West Virginia, page 53
John Brown: Library of Congress
Joseph McCarthy: AP/Wide World Photos

Wisconsin, page 54
Student protests, University of Wisconsin, Madison:
AP/Wide World Photos
Robert LaFollette and grandchild: Library of Congress

Wyoming, page 55
Philip H. Sheridan: National Archives and Records
Administration